A BEGINNER'S GUIDE TO PERSONAL CONSTRUCT THERAPY WITH CHILDREN AND YOUNG PEOPLE

HEATHER MORAN

H J MORAN PUBLISHING

CONTENTS

TECHNIQUES

WRITING ABOUT YOUR WORK

BECOMING EXPERIENCED

RESOURCES - READING AND CONNECTIONS

ACKNOWLEDGMENTS

I have had many interesting discussions with participants at PCP study days and our foundation course which have helped me to think about the topics I might include in this book. I hope I have produced something that could be useful to them.

I want to thank Diane Allen, Peter Cummins and Sally Robbins at the Coventry Constructivist Centre for their continuous encouragement for my PCP work. In particular, Sally has listened to my ramblings and has heard this book developing over the last couple of years. If she hadn't, it probably would not exist. That is a very concrete outcome of PCP coaching. Thanks, Sally!

I have had fantastic support for this project from Penny Thompson, Speech and Language Therapist, Elaine Shone, Educational Psychologist, and Zein Pereira, Speech and Language Therapist. They all read the draft copy and made such helpful suggestions for edits and adjustments. Without them, you definitely would not have had this version as the final draft. Thank you all!

Thanks for the cover photo to Jason Leung at Unsplash.

IS THIS BOOK FOR YOU?

This book is an introduction to using a Personal Construct Psychology (PCP) approach to therapy with young people, written to help those starting out in their journey as a PCP therapist. It begins with issues related to referrals, setting up for therapy (including measuring outcomes) and the initial conversations with young people and the adults around them. Then it moves on to what the PCP therapist would be trying to do in the therapy sessions at the beginning, middle and end of therapy. I have included some useful techniques and there is a section on writing about therapy with examples of letters and the kind of explanations I would give to young people and the adults around them.

This book will not tell you much about PCP theory because it assumes that you already have a little background. If you don't, I hope you will still find it useful and that it might inspire you to learn more about PCP. You will find some useful books and information about PCP training and teaching in the Resources section.

This is intended to be a reference book so the sections are clearly separated, in case you want to find a particular part again. It has made the contents list very detailed but I hope that will be helpful.

My own loose definition of therapy is that it is facilitating work around the way someone understands themselves and approaches their experiences. This could as easily apply to a single consultation if that leads to changes in construing. To me, offering PCP therapy is about helping people to feel comfortable in a more fluid or experimental approach to life or to a problem situation.

I hope that this book can be useful to any professional working to bring about change with young people through any length of therapeutic encounter (single sessions, short- and long-term therapy). I have tried to bear in mind that readers might be drawn from a variety of professions, all of whom are in the business of supporting young people to adjust and/or to make changes in their lives. These professionals might be working in schools, youth services, health services. Typical professions might be psychologists, pastoral and student support staff in schools and colleges, mental health nurses, social workers, speech and language therapists, specialist teachers, youth workers, occupational therapists, counsellors or psychotherapists. If your own profession is not in this list, please don't think that the book will not be useful because I have tried to write it with no fixed profession in mind. My aim was to write something that could help professionals to use a PCP approach in their work. Therefore, if you are interested in PCP and curious about how it might be useful in your work with children, young people and the professionals around them, you already have all that is required. I am assuming that you will keep to your professional standards and that you are reading this so that you can do more work using a Personal Construct Psychology (PCP) approach within those boundaries.

This book will only contain my own views, so I recommend that you also take a look at other authors who have described working with children and adolescents. Please don't be put off by the some of the dates of the publications listed in the Resources chapter - there have been very few books about using PCP with young people.

I hope that you find this book useful and if you do, it would be great if you were willing to offer a review or to comment on the internet. I would like to raise awareness of what PCP has to offer and a review could help with that. If you would like to get in touch with me and tell me how you found my book and please use this email:

drawingtheidealself@icloud.com. You can also let me know other topics I could write about, if you are interested in hearing more from me. I have some ideas but I would really like to know if there is something in particular readers want to see; just bear in mind that this is my preferred style.

If you are interested in arranging a PCP session for you or your team about working with children and young people, parents or teachers, send an email telling me what you are looking for and I will try my best to do something useful.

Heather

ABOUT HEATHER MORAN

I have worked in various settings with young people their families and the professionals around them over the past 40 years. I am a Consultant Child Clinical Psychologist working in the NHS in the UK but I am also an educational psychologist and I practised in local authority services. I teach on the Coventry Constructivist Centre's Personal Construct Psychology foundation course, in occasional workshops and study days and on the Birmingham University doctoral educational psychology training course.

At the beginning of my professional career I worked in a residential special school. Those young people had social, emotional and mental health difficulties and I worked first as a residential social worker and then as a teacher. My husband and I have been specialist foster carers for young people with very difficult behaviour and we have also adopted four children. I have worked with individuals and groups therapeutically and with teams of staff. I want to encourage more interest in PCP so I have written a few papers about my work and I have presented about my PCP therapy and techniques at various conferences. (See my website for details of papers: www.drawingtheidealself.co.uk .)

Personal Construct Psychology (PCP) was devised by George Kelly and published in 1955. It offers a way to understand people and their actions. I found out about PCP early in my career and although I have had training in many other approaches over the years, I have never yet found anything to beat it for versatility. A PCP approach to helps me to understand myself, therapeutic work and organisations. It is not particular to any profession nor to any age group so it has been the backbone of pretty much everything I have done in my working life.

SETTING UP FOR THERAPY

KEY MESSAGES

There are some key messages which underpin everything I have to say about working therapeutically with children and young people, and with the people around them:

- The place the adults and the young person want the *young person* to get to in therapy (and in their life) is probably not exactly the same place.
- The effect of changes in construing may prove to be very uncomfortable, whether those changes are desired changes or not. It will be difficult to anticipate all the implications of any change but this is very important in the process of PCP therapy. It will be important to explore the 'knock-on' effects of changes, particularly in terms of your client's sense of self and the way they might be construed by important others, such as family members and teachers.
- The path to the change is not linear and there will be setbacks and challenges which may lead to distress and disappointment. This does not mean that therapy will not be successful.
- Permanent change takes time to become established so

you might not know the impact of your work, especially if it is a single session.

- The amount of possible change is sometimes surprisingly small or large and this can be difficult to judge at the beginning of therapy.
- You do not know how any particular therapeutic experience might affect your construing of yourself as a therapist and as a person. Be ready to consider how the experience of offering therapy could affect your construing of *your* past and *your* future practice.
- To engage in the process of therapy is to accept that there will be uncertainty in so many respects - for both the client and therapist.

∾

Note: *to help the flow of reading and writing, I will use three terms to represent more possibilities:*

When I refer to 'parents' but parents that can include foster carers, kinship carers (eg. grandparents who are carers), parent's partners etc.

When I refer to 'teacher' but this could be another person in school, such as the person in charge of learning support or pastoral care.

When I will use the terms 'child' and 'young person' fairly interchangeably, without exclusive reference to a particular age group. I might be more specific in parts of the book, but generally I would think that anything I have to say here is relevant to working with younger or older children and adolescents.

REFERRAL ISSUES

Most parents will have well-developed constructs about their child - who they are now and who they are likely to become. They will be construing and reconstruing across the child's development, noticing the things that fit with their anticipations, especially looking out for how the child is in comparison with parents and siblings, or compared with people in the wider family. This can be heard in comments like these:

"He is always hitting the other kids, I don't know why he thinks that is ok in our house."

"She is worrying us all because she is so anxious around people. We have people to our house a lot, and she has never really got better at it."

"His dad was like this and I don't want him to end up the same."

"She is so miserable. My sister was like that at her age and she became really depressed."

As a child grows up, parents will be pointing things out to each other, highlighting growth in some directions and not in others. They might be using a lot of references to others, such as 'like me', 'like you', 'not like us - but like a relative', 'not like any of us - a surprise'. The construing of the family is behind these comments, although they may never have been been fully aware of it. They might not be able to say, for example, "We are the sort of family which thinks/values/avoids/does/never does/is/will never be…"

There are particular problems when a child is developing in ways that lead to the parent feeling uncomfortable (e.g. if a partner was violent and the child looks very like them). Or where the child has an unwelcome condition that is also in the parent (e.g. autism). Or where the child is showing talents for things that the parents do not value (e.g. a child who wants to be a ballet dancer). Parents will not necessarily seek to promote their child's development in a wide way because their own construing will affect the things they determine to be relevant. For example, a parent might not push a child with their school work because they did not do well at school and they do not expect their child to manage the work. Another parent might insist on piano practice because passing music exams helps you to get into the best university.

Where there is more than one child in a family, the child will also be seen in comparison to their siblings. They are likely to find a role in the family, such as "the noisy one", "the sporty one", "the most grumpy". They might be grouped with other siblings in similarity or in contrast: "those two are the arty ones", "she is nothing like her sisters". When we are talking to parents, it is important to find out how they construe their child and their siblings. Ask about what they like to do, how they spend their free time, what they are good at as well as what they struggle with? Ask what they are worried about for this child, what they think might happen if therapy does not help?

It is also helpful to ask parents *who* is concerned about their child? Is it only one parent, is it the grandparents too, is it their teachers, is the child worried? Who is the most worried and why? If things get better, who will be the most pleased? Who or what will be affected most by changes in the child? Will the child's day-to-day life be better and in what way will that affect family life?

～

In a school week, a child typically spends as much time awake at school as at home so teachers and other school staff will be a very important part of a child's life. They will each be using their own construing system to understand and support the child's development. Education systems will have given a set of core constructs to teachers, through the curriculum and the education system's evaluation and monitoring processes, providing a backdrop to what is agreed to be important. These will relate to a range of things such as classroom behaviour, teacher skills, school subjects and progress in each school year.

Some parents will have chosen to remove their child from the usual schooling system temporarily or permanently. They might do this because they disagree with their child being construed (and judged) by the education system, or because they believe the system to be too narrow, or because they want to control the child's experiences. This is an interesting thing to consider - what do parents and child think that they are they gaining or missing out on by not going to school and is that necessarily a good or bad thing?

Other young people will have been excluded by the school, usually related to some kind of risky behaviour (e.g. hurting people) or because of persistent disregard for the school rules. Parental construing will be adjusted to accommodate this experience, e.g. "She can't cope with school", "He has very special needs" or "She has been attacking teachers". These experiences might validate or invalidate their construing of the child, with potential distress for the parent.

Sometimes teachers will be recommending that a young person is given therapy. Such referrals will typically locate the problem within the child. The teacher might say that the child is not achieving their grades (an alternative construction might be "I have not been able to find a way to teach this child what they need to remember"). The teacher might be concerned that the child is so aggressive in class that someone will get hurt (an alternative might be "I can't work out what is upsetting this child so much"). The teacher could refer to the support that has been offered and the fact that the child has not changed as a result (an alternative might be "We haven't found the right way to help him yet"). It will be very important to find out what the implications of change might be. Teachers may recommend a referral but they might not say how they expect therapy will affect the child, their classmates and their teachers. This is always worth asking about. For example: "So, if she is less aggressive in school, who will notice that and what will they see instead? You are her teacher, what will you see? What do you think the other children will notice? Would the head teacher be aware of the change too?" (You may see that some of this style of questioning is also seen in Solution Focussed Therapy but actually it was already in Kelly's PCP.)

The other issue with referrals from schools is related to the amount of change. Is it really possible for a child in school, with little control over what happens during their day, to change permanently? It is more likely that the child might 'slot-rattle', moving to showing the behaviour the teacher wants for a while and then slipping straight back into their old ways (because they are moving between the extremes (poles) of a construct.) We see this happen many times, such as when the shy child performs in the school play but never wants to do it again; when the physically aggressive child has a perfect day in class and there are no fights; or when a child who usually refuses to pick up a pencil produces a beautiful piece of work. Often teachers will construe these experiments by the child as the first day of permanent change and be distressed when their anticipations are invalidated because the child returns to their usual behaviours. They might refer to the fact that the child "*can* do it" meaning that they have seen the child show behaviour which indicates that they do know *how* to behave differently. Perhaps the issue is not whether they can, but whether they keep on doing it, day after day? The 'can do it' also implies that the child is making an active choice not to always 'do it'.

Why might this happen? Perhaps the teacher construes this 'can do it' as invalidating in terms of their competence as a teacher, or as a person, or as a person who is good at working with children? It is important to find out what 'can do it' implies for *this* particular teacher in relation to *this* child. Interestingly, in learning, a teacher would expect that a new skill will only sometimes be shown, e.g. the child might sometimes be able to read a difficult word, depending upon the context and words around it, including their mood, how tired they feel etc. So, what is it about other behaviours and social skills that makes people feel invalidated when behaviour is not always seen? Perhaps a discussion about the development of skill fluency could be helpful to the teacher, so that they feel less threatened by the child's difficulties? If the teacher can reconstrue the problem as a child being unable to show reliably that they have the skills to be consistently good at behaving, then the teacher can be encouraged to be more curious and experimental in their approach to their teaching of *this* child. I will talk more about this later.

S ocial workers are another common source of referrals. They are charged with getting the best for the children they are involved with and their performance in this will be monitored by their managers. The only children to have social workers are those who have faced extreme adversity, including abuse, neglect and disrupted care. This group of young people are likely to have multiple difficulties. Therefore, it might be very helpful to discuss your possible therapeutic input with the social worker before you meet the young person.

It will be important to consider who you might want to involve in your work in the role of parent. The child might be living at home but with active social work supervision of their family. The child who is in care may have a number of people in parental roles with them: a birth parent, a foster carer or a residential care key worker, as well as a social worker. They each might have very different aims and expectations.

PRACTICAL ARRANGEMENTS

It is really important to be clear about who you are and what you do or do not do as a therapist. The commissioner of your work is likely to be the parent or school so you will need to ask about why they are seeking therapy for the child (as opposed to mentoring or some other sort of support). What is their construing of therapy? What do they expect will happen? Have they had therapy themselves? Are they seeking something which is likely to be possible? As a therapist, you will be entering into the construing system of the family. Where might they place you in terms of allegiances? Are you there for the child or for the parents? Are you going to work confidentially or tell them everything that the child says?

It will probably help if you tell the parent/teacher very clearly what they can and cannot expect of you, so they can construe your role more easily. Ideally, this will be available in a written format (on a website or using an information leaflet) so they can see that it is your usual way of working. The information will need to be in writing in case they forget or they do not keep to the boundaries. This probably includes:

- Fee (if applicable) and fee for cancelled sessions

- Length and timings of appointments
- Whether you can allow them to request rearrangements of a therapy session
- When you take calls
- When you read emails
- What contact you will have with school staff
- Confidentiality for the child's sessions
- Confidentiality for the parent's information
- When and how you will report back to the parent
- What will be written at the end of therapy
- Where notes are stored and how long they will be saved for
- Your supervision discussions about the child's therapy

If they want a report at the end, what it will cover, how many copies you will provide, when it will be sent out and what will it cost them (if there is a fee). Remember that writing takes a lot of time and that reports and letters should be considered to be part of a therapeutic intervention. I will come back to the issues around writing later.

DECIDING WHO TO WORK WITH

The young person referred to you may not be the best person to work with. Their referral is the route to getting some help but you will develop a view about what would be most effective. It could be better to work with a young person's parent or teacher, rather than directly with them, or to have a combination of sessions. It will depend upon how the problem is construed and your construction of the possibility of movement.

It might emerge that the young person does not share their parent's views about the problem, nor about the potential benefits of therapy. It can be extremely difficult for parents to get help for their son or daughter when that is the case. You could try offering single sessions, rather than a series. When they attend the second session, you can try to gain agreement for another one. Gradually, the young person's construing of you and therapy might shift enough for you to work really well with them. If they refuse to come at all, you could offer the option of returning at a later date. When I have had such refusals, I have written to the young person after the session to make it clear that they might find they change their mind at some point and if they do, they can ask to come back to see me. In cases where I have done this, some have come back months later but they have been much more prepared to engage.

If the young person is unwilling to come alone but would come with their parent, then you might ask that the parent also attends their sessions, at least for the first few but perhaps for all of them. This could involve them being in the room but separate, as a supportive onlooker, or you might adjust the work to involve the parent and young person.

When children are very young, it makes sense to work with their parent rather than the child, or the parent and child together. This does not mean that working with young children alone is not possible, but that the likelihood of them succeeding to make changes will be even more significantly affected by their context. When I have worked with young children (5-8 yrs), I have usually had parents involved in all their sessions. A parent's presence creates different dynamics but that can be really helpful. I have also facilitated small group therapy sessions with parents and young people together in every session. The interaction between parents, children and a supportive group was an additional benefit. As long as you know what the situation will be, you should be able to tailor your work accordingly.

Where parents have definite views that the young person is heading for some sort of awful future, it will be very important to work with them separately at the beginning of your involvement, aiming to understand their construing without potential harm to their child or their child's therapeutic relationship with you. It is also likely that you would want to try to loosen their construing of the young person's potential future so they can see other possibilities.

This would also be relevant in a school setting. The teacher's constructions of the child will be related to the referral but it could be very unhelpful for the young person to be exposed to the extent of their concern. It would probably affect that young person's construing of themselves, the teacher, the school and of their potential future. It could also validate a young person's view of the hopelessness of their situation, making your job a lot harder.

The question of whom you work with might really be more of a question about the order of when you work with whom. My view is that a referral for a young person will always involve some work with their parents and at least some contact with their teacher. The style and amount of work with these adults will vary from case to case. The following letter and form may be useful to gather information from a school before you meet the young person for the first time.

∼

This is an example of a letter for a school to find out how a young person is getting on there. You could get consent through a call to parents or send it to parents to pass on to the school if they are happy to do that. If you can receive this information by email that is very helpful for speed, but bear in mind that some organisations cannot send information securely. If you are using post, you will need to allow at least a couple weeks for completion and return.

∼

Dear TEACHER NAME
    Re: **CHILD NAME, CHILD DoB, CHILD NHS NUMBER/SCHOOL ID**
    I am THERAPIST NAME, THERAPIST TITLE . CHILD NAME is coming to meet me to see whether I am able to help through therapy or consultations on DATE, TIME. I am contacting you because you know HIM/HER well and it would be really helpful to have your views before our meeting. Parents have given permission for me to contact you.
    I realise that this would be additional work for you but I hope that you will be able to let me have some information about how CHILD NAME gets on in school. I would be hopeful that you might see some changes in school if our work together is successful, so getting a picture now would give me an idea of changes you might hope for.

To help with that, I have enclosed a short, four-question question-naire. It would be very helpful if you could also complete a rating of HIS/HER strengths and difficulties using the Dimensions of Health and Well-being and send the report it creates to me. This will give me an idea of the extent of HIS/HER difficulties. I will be asking parents to use the same tool so that similarities and differences should become clearer.

The website for Dimensions is: https://dimensions.covwarkpt.nhs.uk/Default.aspx

In order to get a picture of CHILD NAME before I meet HIM/HER, it would be extremely helpful if you could send the information to me ahead of my meeting on DATE, TIME. Please send it to the above address or by email to EMAIL ADDRESS.

I will write to you again to let you know the plan for CHILD NAME's work with me after we have met.

Yours sincerely

THERAPIST NAME, THERAPIST TITLE

Cc. Parents

∾

The form below would need a better layout so there is more space for the teacher's responses.

∾

THERAPIST NAME, THERAPIST TITLE
Your name:
Your role and school:
Dimensions report attached? YES/NO
Today's date:

Re: CHILD NAME, CHILD DoB, CHILD NHS NUMBER/ID

1. Relationships

How does CHILD NAME get along with other young people and are you worried about any aspect of HIS/HER interaction with peers and/or adults?

2. Emotions

How does CHILD NAME handle their emotions in school, especially when they are extreme? Does that cause you any concerns about being around HIM/HER when HE/SHE is upset or angry?

3. Responses

How does CHILD NAME respond to being given instructions in school, in a group and individually? Can CHILD NAME accept and respond well to support from school staff at times of difficulty (either with behaviour or academic tasks)?

4. Academic progress

Is CHILD NAME making expected progress with their school work? Are there any difficulties with learning which are affecting achievement? If so, are they all being addressed successfully?

5. What is your most significant concern about CHILD NAME at the moment?

ENGAGEMENT IN THERAPY

At the outset, I would suggest a caution about giving a regular, long term commitment to any client, child or adult. Therapy in PCP will not be driven by any particular protocols or programmes. Therefore, it will be difficult to say how exactly how many sessions it will take, what will happen in them, what tools you might use as part of this, and what the eventual outcome will be. The focus is on reducing distress and developing a sense of self that allows them to engage in their life in a way that makes sense to them. Changes like this that might show in all sorts of ways. So, agreeing to see someone for a smaller number of sessions at a time makes more sense. It also makes it possible to review progress, renegotiate the goals and check with the young person whether they want to continue in therapy. When parents are having to accompany children and young people to appointments, they are likely to want to plan work and childcare around them so giving a short block of appointments might be helpful to them. It is similar in school, where they would need to find a private room and cover staff. In my work, I might fix a block of a few sessions but not be certain at that point who needs to attend each one. That way, parents always expect that you might ask them to attend the next one. Then parents are able to plan their time out of work or their child care arrangements in advance. Of course, in some services, the number of sessions will be determined by capacity rather than the client's need. Then, the task is to work out what might be possible in the therapy time available and to adjust the goals of therapy accordingly.

If it turns out that the young person does not see themselves as in need of therapy, there are three possibilities: change client and work with parents/teachers instead; work on making a relationship with the young person in order to work more therapeutically in the future; or agree to end the sessions. There is little to be gained by repeatedly offering therapy to someone who does not see it as relevant to them.

When young people are very reluctant to attend at all but there is a clear need for help, I might negotiate one session at a time. I explain that I can see that they are running into problems and that my role is to try to help others to know how to help them better. I invite them to try one session, or even one 20 minute session. I would explain that they can stop at any point in the session, or make a decision never to come back for another one. I emphasise their choice in this, and reassure that I won't think badly of them if they decide it is not what they want to do. This usually means that they agree to try one session. If that works, I will go through the same process and ask them to come to another, on the same basis. I do this because I think that some young people have become disillusioned with the effectiveness of previous efforts to help them, especially when they have seen lots of professional helpers. I want them to understand that this will not be the same as past efforts and that their engagement is absolutely key to anything helpful happening in therapy. If that fails, and it sometimes will, I would meet with the parents instead. Once we have reached this point, it seems that I will need to work with what we have, rather than discharge them unless I cannot see any way for me to be helpful within the time constraints we have.

INITIAL CONVERSATIONS

I t will be important to spend some time at the beginning of your therapeutic relationship talking about what therapy is and how it usually progresses. This will help the young person to construe you, the therapy and their responses during the therapeutic process. You will need to make them aware that most changes lead to some discomfort, even when that change is desired. It helps to use an analogy related to the child's interests to help them understand that (e.g. they might want to go to Disneyland in USA even though they hate flying; wearing new trainers might give them blisters but they still want to wear them).

Changes in the young person's construing will also mean that they do or say things which might make other people uncomfortable. The way parents and teachers construe the young person will probably have to adjust and these changes may not be greeted with the delight the young person expects. It is worth making parents/teacher and child aware of this because sometimes changes are in unexpected directions and the adults might think that it is going to make things worse. I remember a child who wanted to invite a bully home for tea and his mum was really not in favour of the visit. The child had started to interact with the bully in a different way and they were getting on better in school. The boy was experimenting by seeing whether the bully would come for tea. His mum was able to adjust her construing enough to do her own experiment by saying yes and the visit worked out well.

There are likely to be points in the therapeutic process when the young person will be feeling less able to manage their feelings. They may show this through distress or irritation. It helps if you can make everyone aware of this in advance. If they can understand that it is a common experience, then the young person may be less upset by their feelings. If you help the young person to anticipate that therapy will not always be an easy road, their difficulties are likely to be experienced in a less threatening way.

One of the issues for young people is that they will need to work in therapy sessions. Although the work is not like school work, they will need to concentrate, consider alternatives, and try things out. This can be mentally and emotionally tiring. Young people (and adults) often arrive at therapy sessions expecting it to be something done *to* rather than *with* them. They can be quite disappointed to find that they will be doing most of the talking and that the answers have to be worked out by them. It can also be an odd experience for them to be asked so genuinely for their views. Young people often expect a teacher-pupil relationship and experience; teachers will guide students towards an answer which the teacher already knows. The questions in PCP therapy will not have prescribed answers and there won't be one 'correct' answer. This can be quite anxiety provoking, especially for those who like to get things right.

You might try using the analogy of a person on a journey to live somewhere they have heard of but do not properly know. The person has not lived there before, although they might have visited the place. They do know that it is *expected* to be a better place than where they live now. However, because they have not lived there, they do not know *how* it will be better to live there until they arrive. The therapist will be on the journey with them but is also unsure of the journey. They have a map that lacks detail. Sometimes, they will go down dead ends and have to accept that they chose the wrong route. Sometimes, they will choose a route with challenges they did

not understand until they were facing them. They will have to experiment, to try out routes and to draw the map as they move forwards.
They will have to work out what went wrong and why, and what
might be better. The therapist is a companion, a co-experimenter
and, at times, could be a guide along some parts of the journey.
However, the final part of the journey to the new home will be taken
by the person alone, without the therapist as a companion but with
all the new understandings of the route. The person will be able to
see the place much more clearly by then and will have imagined
living there permanently, and done some preparation for going it
alone. The therapist may never find out whether they reached their
destination and stayed there, or decided to stop off at an earlier
point, or decided to abandon the final part of the journey altogether.

I t will be necessary to discuss the therapeutic process with the
adults involved with the child, whether these are the parents or
teachers. Their response to the young person will be crucial so it is
important that they develop some understanding. I would discuss
with parents/teacher what changes do they hope to see during and
as a result of therapy? How would they know when things are
getting better? Have they seen someone go through therapy before
and if so, what happened? The purpose of this discussion is to make
sure they know that change is not usually a linear process, with
improvement after improvement. Kelly's Person as Scientist model is
really helpful here. He suggested that people will experiment as they
try out new ways of construing. They will test their constructs,
applying them to new experiences and seeing how they fare. They
will evaluate the results and consider the implications of them. For
example, a child who fears dogs might want to try going near a
small dog. When they do, the dog barks and shocks them. They
confirm their construing of dogs as frightening. If the dog had laid
down and was clearly nervous of the child, their construing of dogs
might have been elaborated so that dogs are not all dangerous. They
have yet to learn that size is little indication of approachability in

dogs, that some dogs are bad tempered or attack when afraid, and that some are very amenable and playful.

Away from the child's hearing, I would ask the adults about the implications of change: who is likely to find changes in the child easy or might find them more of a challenge? For example, what if the withdrawn, shy child starts wanting to go out to play with the children in the street? This would be a new experience for the parents as well, so they would be learning how closely to supervise and whether to allow the child to go into a friend's home.

So, for a parent or teacher, they can expect that their child will make steps forward AND retreat, in a gradual approach which might have diversions and changes in direction as they move forwards. Changes following initial sessions are not necessarily good indicators of eventual progress. What such quick changes may represent is something that has happened before, which is why it is so possible. The adults involved might start celebrating, delighted by the progress, only to be doubly disappointed when the changes do not persist.

Remember that you will have no control over what happens around your therapy sessions, especially before and after them. It will be important to talk to the child's parent or teacher about how they might respond to anxieties around the session. Kelly's definition of anxiety is really helpful here - anxiety is about not having the constructs needed to construe an experience. The assumption made by adults around the child could be that what is happening in the therapy room is leading to the child's discomfort. However, it may be what is happening around it. For example, if the sessions are in school time, what is being missed and how does the child leave their usual lessons to come to their meeting with you? What does the teacher say or do as they go to or return from their session. How do peers react? How does the child explain their absence? What are the arrangements for catching up with the academic work they miss? Do they have to catch up alone or with a teacher? Does catching up have to happen at breaks, affecting their relationships with peers. If you are offering a session after school time, what is the child not doing and how much time does attending really take? If they have to travel to the session by bus with a half hour journey either end, then therapy session will take quite a big chunk of time from the child's free time. If that means there is no time to relax because of others things that need to be done (e.g. homework, shower, dinner), then the child might dread the session. They might be irritable or on edge, worrying about whether they will have enough time to have any fun.

If the young person is missing school to attend an appointment, these same issues are relevant. In particular, how much school time will the child miss? It is very important to maintain school attendance because reduced attendance is clearly linked to increased risk of poorer outcomes for mental health and academic success. I would make it clear at the first appointment that there should be no need to take a day off school to attend an hour's therapy session. Some parents find they have problems getting the child into school later because they are not carried along by their usual routine so allowing the child to have a day off could be easier. However, the child will be at risk of falling behind in learning and will experience disruption to their friendships. This is a significant issue for parents who have to travel on public transport so when possible, it is helpful to try to offer an appointment towards the end of the day.

Another relevant issue is how the young person will come to their sessions - will they be brought? If this means parents taking time out of work, is there a limit to their availability? It will help to know about parents' limitations at the outset so that you can think about whether the work seems to be do-able within their time constraints. If they can take time out for only a few weeks, then I would consider what to work on and how, within the time available.

EXAMPLE EXPLANATIONS

If you are wondering about how to explain Personal Construct Therapy to the person you are going to work with, these examples may be useful. An explanation would not actually be given in a long stream of one-sided talk, but they are here to show how you might include the key messages about what will happen.

Young person - series of sessions

The following explanation could be offered after an initial discussion has made it clear that the work will be with the young person. This is an example for a child with a problem managing their temper.

"So, your parents have been worried about your difficulties with your temper and I can see from what you've said that you are not happy with it either. I can try to help you, if you would like that. The problem with coming to see someone like me is that sometimes it can be a hassle to come (especially if you want to do something else that day) but if you don't keep coming, I won't be able to help you enough because we won't get as much time together. I know people have tried to help with your temper before and that didn't seem to work so you might think that this won't either. You will have to decide whether you are willing to let me try in a different way, after I explain what I would do.

My job is to try to understand things from your point of view so that other people can understand you better and help you in the best way. Although I will be working with you, I won't tell anyone what you say until we have had a discussion about what they need to know and why, and what you agree they can know. This might be a bit frustrating for your mum and dad. The exception is if you tell me that you are being hurt by someone, or that you are going to hurt someone else. Then I would have to tell people so that you or they are kept safe. I also have to write some short notes about our session on our computer records so that my bosses know I am seeing you. At the end of our sessions, I'd like to write a report or letter to send to your parents and teachers so they can understand you better and remember how to help you. We would discuss what will go in that letter in our last session though so we don't need to worry too much about that now.

I have to warn your parents that you might find coming for some help a bit difficult at times. It can be hard work when you have to think a lot. It isn't like school work so it isn't the sort of thing you can get wrong. I have a theory that helps me to work and that is that everyone has their own theories about what they do and why. There is no right or wrong with this, and only you will know your own theories. That's the bit I can help you with - finding out what your theories are and how they work out for you. You might already have some ideas about what doesn't help you and it will be important to discuss those.

If you are willing to come to see me and give it a go, I will do my best to help you. It seems, from what you and your parents have said, that you have had a tough time dealing with your temper. You don't seem to want to get into trouble but it happens. If you are willing to try a couple of sessions and see what you think, then I can give you an appointment to come to see me. If you are not comfortable with our sessions, we will soon know that and we won't carry on if it isn't right for you.

It is important that your parents know that sessions can sometimes make you think a lot and that can be tiring. At your age, you might show this by being a bit irritable or fed up. Also, it might help to not come to our sessions thirsty or starving. I suggest that you get a drink and a snack before you come because you will be able to concentrate better.

So, I won't see you if you don't want to come for my sessions. Realistically, if you are determined that it doesn't suit you, we can think again about what I might be able to do to help you. It is going to be up to you to decide that for yourself. It isn't going to be like school - you don't *have* to come to see me. Sometimes people don't believe that, but it is true. It won't work at all if you feel that you are being 'made' to come. I will try really hard to avoid you having to miss something like your favourite lesson in school or an after school club, but I can't always make that happen.What do you reckon - will you give it a go?"

Young person - single session consultation

This is the sort of explanation that might offered at the start of a single consultation session with a young person.

"So, I am here to see you and I am not sure if you know why? Any ideas? We have only got this one session so we need to get cracking in a minute but it is important that you know how I might be able to help. It seems that lots of people have tried to help you with your temper in school but it hasn't really worked so far. I know that sometimes you get pretty angry and sometimes it has got out of hand. My job is to help other people to understand you - I am not here to tell you off. I reckon you know that it isn't ok and that you don't like it happening either.

Sometimes, when young people meet me, they can be a bit worried about what is going on. I want to try to understand your views and your theories about what happens and then explain that to other people, so they can help you better. It is important that you tell me as honestly as you can. We will have an agreement at the end about what can be said to other people - you might tell me something you don't want them to know for some reason. The only bit I have to let you know now is that if you tell me that you are being hurt or you are going to hurt other people, I will have to talk to other people about that because there are rules about that sort of thing.

We have got about an hour and then that's it - I won't be seeing you again. Usually, I have to write something for the school at the end. We can talk about that later because I'd want you to know what I'll write and I won't know that until we get to the end of our discussion. They will need something in writing so that they remember what I have said about your views. You will be able to have a copy if you want one.

I have some ideas about how we can get started, if you are ok with that?"

Joint parent and child - series of sessions

This sort of explanation would be for working with young person *and* their parent. The example is for a mum but it could be one or more parents/carers of any gender.

"So, from what you and your mum have said, you have been having problems keeping your temper under control and I know from what you have both said that this is quite a problem at home. So, I could try to help by meeting with you and your mum. I know that you have seen a couple of people before and that it didn't seem to help much so you might both be feeling a bit fed up at the thought of doing something like that again. I will try to do it in a different way because it seems that the missing part is a really good understanding of your views. So my job is to understand your views, help you to work out what you think will help, and see if there is a way to do things better in future. This is so you don't keep trying things that don't work well enough.

I can meet with you for a couple of sessions and then with your mum for a couple of sessions. Then we'd meet together again. If you're really not happy to come into the room without your mum for a session, she can come in too. I don't want to make it hard for you. I might have to ask her to keep pretty quiet in your session - will that be hard for her? I would still want to have a chat with your mum on her own for a couple of sessions though, if she is ok with that.

There is something important that you both have to know. When we are having our discussions, if you tell me that you are being hurt or that you are going to hurt someone else, then I will have to talk to someone else about that so that people are kept safe. I would talk to you about it first though.

The other thing that really matters is that I can't really help you unless you want to come and give it a try. If you don't think that there is even a chance this might help, then it's probably not going to work. I would rather you said that and then we can think about what else could be done. I know it will be hard for your mum to fit these appointments into a busy family life, so we don't want to fix up something that both of you don't want to come to. I am sorry but I will have to give you the appointments I have available, so they might not fit perfectly into your school or work times. If there is a definite day and time to avoid, you can say so and I will see what I can do.

So, the question is, do you want me to set something up with you?"

~

Parent consultation session

This sort of explanation is for the beginning of a consultation with a parent.

"I wanted to meet with you to get a good idea of what you think is happening with Billy's temper problems. As his mum, I am sure you will have thought about it a lot and by now you'll have some theories about how it has developed and why it happens. I am not trying to find someone to criticise because I reckon that most parents try to do their best job at parenting and some kids are trickier than others, even for experienced parents. The aim is to think what could help him more in the future.

Sometimes at the start of the discussion, parents think that they have no idea why something happens and what might help, but actually it can become clearer as we discuss it. There are some things I want to ask you about in particular, and I might need to bring us back on track if we wander away in our discussions. I know you have seen other people about Billy before so some of what I ask about might seem a bit different.

Are you are ok with that?"

Teacher consultation session

This explanation could be offered to a teacher at the start of a single consultation session.

"Ok, so I am meeting with you to talk about the problem Billy has with his temper. I want to have a chat about the kind of things that happen and what you think is going on. I know you have sent information in the referral and in the questionnaire I gave you but I also want to get a feel for what it is like to have him in class with you. The aim is to understand your views so that I can think about what might be useful to do next - or what should be avoided. I have to ask you a few questions about what happens when things go wrong, and when it might be fine. I know that by now, you have probably thought a lot about it, so it is great that we can meet. As someone who is with him a lot, you will probably have your own theories about what is going on. It would be good to find out about these as we go along."

ABSENCE LETTER TO TEACHER

I t is very important that young people are able to attend their therapy sessions. Therefore, some sort of communication with school staff will support their attendance. The following is an example of a letter to explain their absence. It might help to send this kind of letter to the school when you have arranged your sessions. It includes a request for their support around attending therapy.

~

D ear <TEACHER NAME>
Re: <CHILD NAME>, CHILD DoB>, <CHILD ID/NHS No.>

I am <THERAPIST NAME, THERAPIST TITLE> . <CHILD NAME> is going to be attending therapy sessions with me at <CLINIC>, starting on <DAY> at <TIME>. The aim of these sessions if to help <NAME> with <PROBLEM>. This will mean that <CHILD NAME> cannot be in school between these times: <PICK_UP TIME to DROP OFF TIME> on <DAY>. At the moment, I cannot be sure how many weeks <NAME> will need to attend for. It is unfortunate that <CHILD NAME> will miss school at these times but it is important. Please could you let parents know the arrangements for <CHILD NAME> to catch up with the work they will miss?

It would be helpful if you could let me know if you have particular concerns about <CHILD NAME> during their therapy. Progress in therapy probably will not be continuous and changes are likely to be small and gradual. Sometimes, there will be particular challenges and <CHILD NAME> may struggle. I will be keeping in touch with parents so please let them know if you notice any changes.

It will be important that you have a conversation with <CHILD NAME> about <HIS/HER) absence from school lessons and how <CHILD NAME> would like you to help them to leave comfortably at the appointed time and come into their lessons after they return. Children can be sensitive about their sessions with me so please do not refer to the reason for their absence directly when in front of other students and staff.

Yours sincerely

<THERAPIST NAME, THERAPIST TITLE>

Cc. Parents

MEASURING CHANGE

BEING A CREDIBLE THERAPIST

I have placed this chapter here because I recommend that you to give it some thought before you start. I recognise that this might be a bit dull so please don't let it stop you reading the rest of the book! It is important to consider what you will use to evaluate your therapy. This chapter will focus on measuring at three points in time in the therapeutic encounter: before you start your sessions, in the initial phase and in the final stage. It will also emphasise the need to have something that measures progress as you go through the sessions, in terms of the young person's progress and your ability to connect with them successfully (the therapeutic relationship).

For your own credibility as a therapist, you need to be able to say whether someone has improved over time. How will you know that the client (a parent or child) is better than they were? They will be able to tell you but sometimes they will need help to tell you clearly. If you have completed some baseline assessments or questionnaires, you will be able to look back at the results and make comparisons. You will probably find it helpful to collect both qualitative data (i.e. they report feeling and being better in their sessions) *and* quantitative data (i.e. they score at a different place on some sort of questionnaire or rating scale). Using both kinds of data, your credibility as a therapist is likely to be enhanced. It is very important to measure change in therapy in a personal and meaningful way and in PCP there are some helpful techniques which can run alongside any norm-referenced questionnaire or assessment.

COLLECTING INFORMATION BEFORE
YOUR FIRST SESSION

Before you can measure progress, you will need a clear idea of what the problem is and how 'bad' it is. This will come from discussions and information from the young person and parent and, typically, their teacher too. It may also include questionnaires and assessment tools. To me, it makes no sense not to seek information from the two places the child spends most of their time: home and school. Sometimes, I have sought information from activity club leaders too. It is difficult without information from a school because you would only have the parent's construction of how the child is in school. That will not be as helpful (nor as accurate) as hearing it from the teacher. One person in school might need to collate the views or a number of teachers and support workers. Of course, parents and/or the young person will need to consent to information being sought from school and it may not be possible to negotiate that until your first meeting with the family.

If the child is not causing concern in both places, it will be interesting to explore that later. Kelly drew attention to the importance of exceptions - times when or places where the presenting problem does not occur. Knowing about exceptions will only be possible if information is collected, ideally through a conversation with someone in school who knows the young person well. You will hear some of the teacher's construing much more clearly in a phone call than when a questionnaire is completed. However, I suggest that a minimum would be to write to the teacher and tell him/her that you are working with the young person and invite them to tell you about how they get on in school or send them a questionnaire to complete. For most young people, the key areas to ask about are their ability to manage their emotions, their relationships and interactions with peers, their school work and their response to adults in school. School work is relevant whatever the referral is for, particularly in terms of attitude to learning.

In contrast, if the referral is from school and the meetings with the young person will be there, the additional information will need to be sought from parents, even if the problems are only seen in school. This could be done to some extent in a meeting with the teacher present but you might not find out how parents construe the school and teacher if they are all seen together. The parents' construing is likely to be clear to their child so if they are very unhappy, you need to know that, if you are working to try to improve things at school.

There is a section below outlining some free tools to use. In my opinion, there is no need to buy any but there are many question-naires for sale from various test providers if you need something different.

BASELINE TOOLS

I t will be important to consider using tools to provide a baseline during your initial sessions (something often thought of as an assessment phase but PCP does not make that division). The use of measures might help you with your formulation. A baseline is a starting point: at this point in time and understanding, what are the child's problems?

The UK-based **Child Outcomes Research Consortium (CORC)** is an organisation which supports the use of data collection and analysis in child and adolescent mental health. Their website contains details of many assessment and outcome measures: https://www.corc.uk.net/outcome-experience-measures/.

In Coventry and Warwickshire Partnership Trust, in the UK, we have developed a free web-based tool called **Dimensions of Health and Well-Being**: https://dimensions.covwarkpt.nhs.uk/Default.aspx. This may be used by parents and professionals working with young people and it can be repeated any number of times. The tool creates a report based on the ratings given on 28 aspects of social and emotional development which have been found to affect resilience and vulnerability to mental health problems (e.g. worrying and anxiety, sleep, relationships with parents/carers). The report contains useful links to self care information available through UK and online self-help organisations, and also to videos, apps, websites, reading material and books. A Dimensions rating might be useful at the start and end of your therapy but it is also a useful resource to pass on to parents and teachers so they can find information to help them support their child. Web browsers will allow translation of websites so Dimensions should be useable in other countries.

If you are finding out how a young person is in school, you can also ask the teacher to complete Dimensions rating as part of that. This would provide a broad picture and additional information could be provided as appropriate.

INITIAL FORMULATION

B y the end of your first session, you will need to end up with an initial summary and simple formulation. As therapy proceeds and understanding increases, the formulation will be adjusted. Therefore, the initial formulation will need to be tentative and may only apply until the next session. Therefore, it would not be very detailed. You will only be able to formulate through the lenses of your own construing. A PCP formulation would make reference to construing so if it is written, you would see a difference in the language used, as in this example.

A typical non-PCP formulation might be:

Billy has problems with his temper. He is easily annoyed and there are daily outbursts of physical aggression towards parents and siblings. Billy does say that his reactions are not good for him, nor for other people. He says that he wants to develop better self control. Since babyhood, Billy has always struggled to contain his anger. He does control himself better at school and it is not clear why this is.

An initial formulation in PCP therapy might look more like this:

Billy reports that he has problems with his temper and he is asking for help to change. We are not sure why it happens but he feels threatened easily and he expresses this by shouting and hitting other people. His parents construe him as angry and aggressive and have done since babyhood. He has always had this problem at home but in school it happens less often, suggesting that he construes himself differently in the two environments.

Whatever the initial formulation is, it will probably change considerably over the course of therapy, as your understanding of the child and their context increases. As a PCP therapist, your focus is on the child's sense of self, something we will gradually find out more about through our work with them. It is also about how the adults construe the child. The final formulation might be very different from the initial one because at the start, you will not have much more than your own construing to use to predict what that might look like. You will not know what changes might occur in the child's own construing, in the way they are construed by others, and in the way they are construed by you as therapist. Your construing will be based upon our initial exploration with the child and parent/teacher, your own experiences, and your sense of self as a therapist.

Therapy in PCP will not be driven by any particular protocols or programmes. Therefore, it will be difficult to say how many sessions it will take, what will happen in them and what the eventual outcome might be. Your focus is on facilitating adjustments in construing that could lead to reduced discomfort and finding ways forward that fit with *that* individual young person. Progress could show in all sorts of ways. In Billy's case, you might expect that your work will lead to fewer episodes of hitting his siblings but it will not necessarily work out as simply as that. It could be that Billy decides to explore that aspect of himself more and take up boxing. Gradually, over a period of weeks, he moves his hitting from the home situation to the boxing club. This might never have been considered as a possible intervention at the start of therapy because the emphasis was on stopping something. As therapy progresses, joining a boxing club becomes a possible experiment and it works out well. The problem with controlling his temper is addressed in a way that makes sense to Billy. Hitting siblings at home is reduced but overall expertise in hitting is greatly increased. Often, parents and teachers will have thought a lot about what 'getting better' means. However, their 'better' will not necessarily be the way it works out, or the path to that 'better' might not be what they expect.

MEASURING PROGRESS ACROSS SESSIONS

For you to be sure you have done a good job, you need to find ways for the child (and/or a parent or teacher) to tell you that things are better, and how they are better. Then you would probably want to to check that out with adults around them (e.g. asking their parents and teacher whether they have noticed any changes). This qualitative data can also be provided through the child's own rating scales or grids.

Personal goals and rating scale

As PCP therapist, the most significant measure would be something that has been designed by the young person - something that shows a view of self and a view of ideal self. You could use my own technique for this **Drawing the Ideal Self technique:** www.drawingtheidealself.co.uk. The technique is easy to use and has been tried and tested in many situations by myself and other professionals. It is free to use and does not need any special equipment. There are other useful PCP tools available which can be found in these books:

Ravenette (1990): Personal Construct Psychology In Educational Psychology Practice. A Practitioner's View

Butler and Green (2007):The Child Within: Taking the Young Person's Perspective by Applying Personal Construct Psychology.

Session by session rating scales

There are rating scales which are designed to be used at the start and end of every session. These were developed by Scott Miller. They are very simple tools to measure the effectiveness of therapy from the client's viewpoint. They are free for the paper version and you can use these for work with children, young people and adults, as well as individuals or groups. It only takes about two minutes to complete each one. Scott Miller's website can be viewed here: https://scott-d-miller-ph-d.myshopify.com/collections/performance-metrics/products/performance-metrics-licenses-for-the-ors-and-srs).

At the beginning of every session, Miller's **Child Outcome Rating Scale (CORS)** is completed. This invites the young person to rate themselves over the past week. It includes ratings of self, family, school and an overall rating.

The **Session Rating Scale (SRS)** is used at the end of every session as an evaluation of the effectiveness of your therapeutic engagement with that young person. It invites the young person to rate whether they felt that you listened to them, whether you and they talked about important things, whether they would like to do something similar next time and then they give an overall rating for the session. The SRS is a therapy evaluation tool for the child and a chance to provide you with direct feedback about your session.

These rating scales are very easy for a child to use and there are different versions for younger and older children. The ratings can lead to a discussion about the style of the session so that you can adjust the way you facilitate your sessions to suit the client. Although you cannot score these digitally without buying a licence, nor use them in a digital format, that is not necessary if you do not want to look at a total dataset. You can simply make a paper chart on which to record the results. The digital version would allow you to do more with your data from clients (e.g. compare yourself in therapy with different clients or track the progress of your clients as a group).

Tracking problems and symptoms

You can find out more about outcome measures on the **Child Outcomes Research Consortium (CORC)** website: https://www.corc.uk.net/outcome-experience-measures/outcome-rating-scale/.
This website also has information about what are called symptom-trackers. These are very short questionnaires to be completed at the start of a session but they each have a specific focus (e.g. OCD symptoms, anger). Using these allows you to look at specific symptoms and see how therapy affects them.

Dimensions of Health and Well-Being provides a wider view because it takes the child's context into account (https://dimensions.covwarkpt.nhs.uk/Default.aspx). Dimensions is better completed by adults or older young people and could be used at the start and end of therapy. You might find that change does not show well on some mental health/illness measures but it does show on Dimensions. For example, if a young person is still feeling anxious regularly but they have started to go to a football club with a group of friends, then the change would not show on an anxiety symptom tracker but might show really clearly on Dimensions and on the young person's Drawing the Ideal Self rating scale.

Remember that the purpose of measuring outcomes is to show the value of what you do. The most effective measurement will involve a combination of different measures so that there is something very personalised, something about individual sessions and something about changes in the problems which led to your involvement. Using outcome measures will never be a waste of time and looking at trends in your data will help you to see the value of your own work. Sometimes, it can feel that you are getting nowhere in your therapeutic work, perhaps with an individual but also if you have a number of 'stuck' clients. I have often been cheered up by looking at a chart of progress because I was feeling stuck too. Looking back at changes and noting what worked last time is not something reserved for clients - therapists need to do it too!

A PERSONAL CONSTRUCT THERAPY PROCESS

PRACTICE STEMS FROM PCP THEORY

The essential style of PCP therapy relates directly to the theory. It suggests that the therapist takes a curious stance in relation to the client, whatever their age and problem. In work with children and young people, this might be a surprise for them. The PCP therapist is extremely interested in their views, wants to explore them and accepts them as genuine. No views are determined to be right or wrong, even when they might seem to lead a person into trouble. The expert on the client is taken to be the client, at any age. This person has their own understandings of their world, based upon their experiences. They live their own lives, even when they are young. The job of the therapist is to understand and accept their personal constructions as their own version of themselves and their life. This is what being credulous means.

For example, you might assume that a child's tendency to argue with other children is related to wanting to dominate their interactions because they have been reported as "bossy" by parents and teachers. The child might provide a different view: they explain that this is about helping other children: "When I know what to do, I tell the others so they can do it straight away." That construction of themselves as 'helpful' is important to them. Therapeutic input is likely to be more successful if the therapist is able to elaborate that construction and understand all the ways the child sees themselves as helpful. Therapy might involve trying to assist the child in finding ways of being helpful without irritating the other children and adults. That might require some social skills teaching about possible ways to offer help to peers. In PCP terms, this input is around sociality. The child will be more able to construe another's construing so that they will be more successful in being helpful. The therapist also needs to develop sociality because they need to be able to construe the young person's constructions and take the role of therapist with them.

There is no one way to 'do' PCP therapy, no process that 'must' be followed. The intention is to explore construing and to facilitate reconstruction in such a way that the young person can get on with their life more comfortably. This does not mean that it doesn't matter what is done or that anything goes in PCP therapy, but rather that there is plenty of space for difference and experimentation. Therapy would not follow the same process each time because every person needs their own version of therapy even when the aim might be very similar.

Let's take the example of therapy for addressing a fear of dogs. The key is to find out what that fear is about and to work with the underlying constructions. For one young person it might be that they have been bitten by a dog. For another, they might be more generally anxious and dogs are the latest fear in a long list. Another might only be afraid of dogs when they are not on a lead. The behaviour of these individuals might look pretty similar to an observer in a park where dogs are being walked. They might all run screaming to their parent and hide behind them. Observation alone would not be able to identify the reasons for their behaviour.

My own experience of observing the behaviour of children and young people in schools or other settings is that it can lead to me being none the wiser about cause. I can guess at causes but that is as far as it goes. I would want to have a conversation about what they were doing and about why it made sense to them at that time. Interestingly, classroom observations are often followed up by practitioners with a discussion with a teacher rather than a child. This can be very useful as an exploration of the teacher's constructions of the young person and of the situation but says very little about the child's constructions. However, if therapists (most typically those who are psychologists or behaviour specialists) make a classroom observation it can be really helpful as part of preparation or information collection, setting the scene for follow up discussions. It could prove to be rather worrying for the teacher because they will risk their construing of the child being invalidated by a one-off observation.

It is likely that the teacher will want to involve support services when she has reached the end of her tether and therefore may already be feeling vulnerable. My own experience of carrying out observations of children who are referred because they misbehave is that at the time of the observation, they usually behave really well or no worse than others in the class. Seeing their 'problem child' behave well might not help the teacher apart from showing her that there are exceptions (i.e. that her construing of the child as 'always naughty' seems to be too tight). However, she will probably already know that.

This does not mean that an observation is not a helpful way to find out more about the child, their context and the teacher, but data from an observation may not fit with the teacher's concerns. If the child is angelic, will that tell us more than careful questioning could have discovered? My argument is related to PCP theory - children are not referred because of their behaviour per se. They are referred because of the meaning their behaviour has to the referrer. I have been in many classrooms where there are children behaving in more challenging ways than the referred child. That makes for an interesting conversation afterwards - why have they not been referred and why was the target child referred rather than them? It could be that the other children have only just started to be a challenge, or that the teacher is confident that she can address their problems without need for outside advice. The teacher might have taught the referred child earlier in their school years and can see that the problems have not reduced so she sought the referral. Reasons for not making a referral can be very useful in your efforts to understand that teacher.

Causal factors identified by the young person and their parents or teacher will lead to the aims of the therapy sessions. It is important to find out from the child and parents/teachers how they think the current problem arose (i.e. their theories of causation). Without that, you might offer something that they think is irrelevant. For example, in the three dog fear examples above, the first conversations would include asking about what they see as the causes of the fear. This would lead to some detailed discussions and then an agreement about what seems to be the most helpful way forward.

The young person who has been bitten might need some work around the traumatic event. Therapy could be focussed on understanding the way that child has been affected by the dog bite in terms of their construing of self, their construing of dogs. The more generally anxious child might need some work with parents first so that they can develop constructions of their child as able to manage their own anxiety levels. The young person with fear of dogs on the loose might be helped by reading dog behaviour so that they can become a better judge of risk.

PCP therapy requires the therapist to be creative in their selection of tools and techniques so that they are useful for working with that young person. It also means that young person does not 'fail' in therapy - a relief for young people who have often had so many problems and failed interventions before they reach their PCP therapist. The therapist holds the responsibility for tailoring the therapy and adjusting the style to fit the young person. If it is not working, that is the therapist's responsibility to work out why and what might work better.

It is also the therapist's business to know what they are doing and how it relates to the theory, but PCP theory does not need to be understood in any detail by the young person. They do need to know that there are different kinds of therapy and that PCP therapy is one which might well suit them because it is suitable for difficult problems. However, they also need to know that if they have a strong view that they should be having another model of therapy, then they could be referred on (unless you are able to provide that model as well). To date, although I have offered to refer on, it has not been needed, but I have had some very shaky starts in PCP therapy.

The most difficult starts seem to have happened more when there has been previous CBT which the young person found very helpful at the time of therapy. Typically, they have been taught well and known exactly what to do in CBT terms. They have understood the elements of a CBT formulation and they can talk through the strategies. What they have struggled with is 'going it alone'. They have not been able to accept that managing their symptoms could be an ongoing part of their future life. The young person's sense of self has been the issue - seeing their 'symptoms' as somehow separate from their personhood. My role in therapy has to been to work with them to address this but the initial phase has been quite uncomfortable because I did not provide the expected style of support. That is, I did not tell them what to do next in the management of their problem. I did invite them to consider a number of possibilities and helped them to generate their options. If you saw the Session Rating Scales from the start of their therapeutic encounter with me, you would notice that their ratings of therapy with me were not high but they were honest! Gradually, they increased. To me this was about the young person getting used to quite a different style of therapy and we needed to have a lot of conversations about what their ratings represented. Using the scales was a helpful process for focussing our attention on making therapy sessions more therapeutic for these young people. In each case, the eventual outcome has been very good, with young people getting on with their lives and being able to understand themselves as a person who has to keep an eye out for how they respond to stress or to insufficient selfcare. They know that this has been important in the development of their sense of self and that it is possible not to define themselves by their difficulties.

The purpose of PCP therapy is to understand how someone has become stuck in experiences that cause them discomfort or distress. This will relate to their construing of their own experiences and of themselves. They could be doing things they may not 'want' to do but find themselves doing repeatedly (e.g. hitting their mum); or they are thinking things that cause them a problem (e.g. "I don't want to go to that horrible school"). The therapist's role is to try to help the young person to understand how and why it happens, and why is is not 'irrational' or 'crazy'. In the process of increasing understanding, potential solutions are likely to emerge.

One of the important features of PCP is that it does not focus on us satisfying desires or needs. This might be the case for behaviour therapy where the 'function' of the behaviour is the focus. PCP is about how it makes sense to that individual to stick with repeating experiences rather than try new ones. It is about a person's meaning-making - the way they make sense of their experiences. It is expected that two people being in the same place at the same time will not have the same experience. The therapist's job is to discover the individual's constructions and how they link together with other ways they construe experiences.

For example, the therapist could be trying to find out how and when it makes more sense for a child to hit their mum than not to hit their mum when they get angry with her. It has to be related to the way the young person construes themselves and others. Perhaps they are 'the sort of child who is unable to control themselves when they are angry'. Perhaps they construe their mum as 'someone who will be hit and still want a relationship with me'. In PCP theory, Kelly did not separate out behaviour and thinking (as Cognitive Behaviour Therapy does) - construing does it all. If a child construes school as a frightening place, their behaviour in relation to school will be in keeping with that construing (perhaps by crying when they arrive). Construing leads to behaviour and behaviour leads to construing. You can see this when thinking about little children. They are unlikely to have a construction of themselves as frightened of dogs until a dog frightens them and they run away. They did not know they could be scared by a dog. It is the same with choosing a biscuit from a selection - the child tries a chocolate one, finds they like it and then becomes a child who likes chocolate biscuits.

PCP therapists are facilitators of therapy - they are on that journey with their client but it is the client's journey and the client will have to take charge of a number of aspects of it. For young people, this is likely to be a very odd experience. They are used to adults telling them what to do, how to do it and what it should achieve. Young people are also used to being told that adults hold the answers and they have to get their answer as close to the adults' answer as possible. A PCP approach can tolerate any answer and accept it - the young person's view will not be 'corrected' by their therapist. The therapist will find it interesting and will be considering how other known constructions might be linked. They will also be looking out for the child's most important theories (i.e. core constructs).

THE IMPORTANCE OF FINDING OUT
ABOUT CORE CONSTRUCTS

A really important part of PCP therapy will be to find out about core constructs. They are the reason the young person does things. Knowing what some of their core constructs are will help the therapist to anticipate the way the young person might respond to their experiences. A lot of PCP techniques will help the therapist to find out about core construing. There is no limit to the number of core constructs a person has but there are likely to be a smallish number. They will often include constructs to do with family, spirituality / religion, friendship, work, play, illness and death. Have a look at these examples and consider how these constructs might affect the way a person approaches life. Remember that constructs have two poles and the two poles are the extremes on a continuum. In conversation, you will be offered one pole and have to ask for the contrast with questions like "What is the contrast to that? Or "As opposed to...?" Or "Rather than...?" In each example below, the pole of the construct the person came up with first is on the left (i.e. the emergent pole). These examples use the same areas of construing for the purpose of illustration of personal construing - family, religious belief, friendship, work, play, illness and death.

Here is an example set of core constructs from Christine:

- Family is important and those relationships should be protected vs. Family is irrelevant
- There is no god vs. God tells me what to do
- Friendship is a two way process vs. Friendship can be one-sided
- Work is something to be tolerated vs. Work is fun
- Play is fun vs. Play is only for young kids
- Illness and death are inevitable vs. Immortality is possible.

Here are Melana's core constructs:

- Family is a place of misery vs. Family is loving and supportive
- God will judge me vs. God doesn't mind what I do
- Friendships are useful vs. Friendships are a frivolity
- Work is to get money vs. Work is satisfying
- Play is for children vs. Play is for adults
- Illness and death are terrifying vs. Unafraid of pain.

Here are John's core constructs:

- Family is unpredictable vs. Family is stable
- Pleasing God is important vs. Pleasing God does not matter
- Friends are better than family vs. Family is the most important relationship
- Work is a way to please God vs. God does not mind what work I do

- There is a time and place for play vs. Playing all the time
- Illness can be a punishment from God vs. Illness is self-inflicted
- Death is relief from suffering vs. Death is unwelcome.

Looking at these, consider how each of these people might respond to hearing that a friend is ill? They will act according their construing. Christine might go round to see them and offer help because friendship is a two-way process. Melana might do nothing more than send a card. John might be very upset by the news and go straight round to see them and pray with them.

How they might they react to being invited to attend the christening of her best friend's baby? Christine might attend for the sake of their friend even though it is a religious ceremony. Melana and John will probably attend without question because they have religious beliefs. Although their behaviour is similar, their construing and the reasons for their actions are different.

What about if they find they have cancer? Christine might accept it and not be too distressed. Melana might be very afraid and go straight to a counsellor for help. John may be devastated and worry about what he has done to deserve such punishment by God.

For each of their core constructs, Christine, Melana and John could rate themselves along it and say how much it applies to them, most of the time. For example, in relation to his own family, John might rate himself here:

Family is unpredictable —x——— Family is stable

It is more tolerable to adjust construing about something that is not a core construct. Often in therapy, you will be looking out for how constructs are connected. They might all shift together or be able to move separately. For example, if John had experiences that led to him seeing family as stable, how might that affect his construing of himself on the other core constructs. His construing of friendships might also change.

In your therapeutic work with the young person, you would need to look out for their core constructs. One way to discover core constructs is through laddering a construct. You can find out more about that in the Techniques section.

THE INITIAL PHASE OF THERAPY

P CP does not separate out assessment and intervention phases in therapy. This might seem odd because in the early phase you might use various tools and techniques to help you to clarify problems. However, these methods will also help the young person to understand their own construing, and that awareness can lead to them making some changes. What you will not know at the start of your encounter with a young person is when and how that might happen. It could be that you ask a question or use a technique in the initial phase of therapy that illuminates something they were less aware of. Kelly does not use terms such as unconscious - he calls this a lower level of awareness of construing. The role of the therapist is to help the young person to become more aware of their constructions. For example, questioning about times the problem does not occur can shift a young person's construing of the problem as being constant. This might lead to a change in the way s/he sees themselves, opening up the possibility of acting differently.

However, particularly in the early phase of a therapeutic encounter, whether it is expected to be a single session or more, there will be a role for the use of techniques to explore construing. This can be through conversational processes or through the use of techniques which involve drawing, writing or any other method. The therapist is trying to understand the construing of the young person and can use whatever suits that young person. For some, drawing would be useful, for others, doing would be better. Finding the right way for that individual young person is the job of the therapist so you will need to have some techniques at the ready. Fortunately, there are clear explanations of a number of suitable techniques freely available in books and websites. There are some links in the Resources section of this book. However, do not be afraid to make up your own. The PCP community is very accepting of new techniques and Kelly was always clear that the PCP theory and techniques would evolve. So, if you love to use particular materials, why not try something out and see where it takes you. As long as the technique will illuminate construing and is useful for that, it is likely to be helpful. I would strongly encourage you to find a way to share those techniques through PCP networks and wider. What you find useful might really help someone else in their work.

Particularly in this initial phase, you will be trying really hard to get a clear picture of the problem. Any techniques you use will be chosen to help you to ask the questions in a relevant format and to help the young person to answer them. Kelly's seven questions are below. Although the language is too formal and rather old fashioned (because they are from 1955) they are easily translated into more modern language. Kelly said:

"The formulation of the questions is designed to get the client (1) to place the problems, if possible, on a time line, (2) to see them as fluid and transient, and then to interpret them as responsive to (a) treatment, (b) the passing of time and (c) varying conditions." (Kelly, 1991, Vol 2, p. 283).

"A. Upon what problems do you wish help?

B. When were these problems first noticed?

C. Under what conditions did these problems first appear?

D. What corrective measures have have been attempted?

E. What changes have come with treatment or the passing of time?

F. Under what conditions are the problems most noticeable?

G. Under what conditions are the problems least noticeable?"
(Kelly 1991, Vol 2, p. 282).

In the initial phase of therapy, question A is hugely important, especially in work with young people who are unlikely to have sought the referral and may not have properly consented to it. The techniques you use will have to find out whether there is any work to be done in therapy with this young person at the moment. If they do not see themselves as having a problem, or they acknowledge the problem but do not share the referrer's interest in addressing it, then talking therapy is not the going to be the way forward. Instead, it could be useful to get a good idea about the way the young person construes him/herself and their personal ambitions. You might then consider switching to work with the adults around the young person since they are seeking change and might be more willing to work on it.

Questions B and C are very interesting. It can be really helpful to ask for the earliest memory of the problem being present. If a parent is present, ask about whether there was any sign of it in babyhood, then toddlerhood - often there were. This is to get an idea of what you could be dealing with. If the problem has always been there, you are facing a very tough job in therapy and might need more discussion to explore ideas around the possibility of change. If the problem has arisen later, then they might have theories of how it has arisen and they are likely to have a previous construction of life without the problem.

Asking about previous attempts to address the problem (D & E) is very important but in the initial phase it is just to find out more about the problem and its resistance to efforts to get rid of it. Typically, young people initially say that they have done nothing and that the adults have been coming up with all the strategies. Often young people seem to have become separated from their difficulties, but it is likely that they have tried to do something about it.

Questions F and G are about when, where and how problems occur. They often show up some interesting factors. Pay particular attention to when problems only occur in relation to particular people or situations (e.g. bedtime, in the maths lesson, inside the home). These are all things to come back to and understand better later and find out more about. Often there are young people who have problems only in school or at home and this difference has been accepted by the adults without much question about how and why that is the case.

The initial phase is about getting sufficient understanding of the young person's views to decide what to do next.

THE MIDDLE PHASE OF THERAPY

The middle phase of therapy might be 30 minutes in the middle of an hour's session with a young person if that single consultation is the only session or it could be 4 sessions if there are six planned sessions. Sometimes there is very little middle because understanding the problem takes a lot of time but then quickly leads to solutions. My experience of this fits well with Kelly's premise that is does not make sense to separate assessment from therapy - PCP therapy involves constantly assessing, always with the potential to be therapeutic.

During PCP therapy the young person will be going through cycles of working through problems by understanding them better, discussing potential alternative constructions of those problems, talking about how other experiences and constructions interact, and experimenting with reconstructions.

This phase is about trying out possibilities in the therapy session. Kelly's idea of how therapy proceeds is to 'try on' constructs in the therapy sessions before experimenting with them in the outside world. This means talking through situations using a propositional position: what if ..., supposing that..., what might happen if...? This means that the client is with the therapist at the time they realise there could be some significant implications of changes they might make. The therapist can then present possibilities they might not have considered.

For example, a young person who is always in trouble in school then has a great lesson with their English teacher, what will the teacher make of that and how might it be construed by the other students in the class? The young person needs be helped to see that there are many possible outcomes from their good behaviour and each one will lead to something else. What if the teacher does not even notice? What if their friend thinks they have become boring? What if the teacher expects this every day afterwards? What if the young person finds that they can't do the work even when they listen and engage well? What if they turn out to be good at English?

These things need consideration before the experiment takes place so that the results are not too much of a surprise and the young person has some strategies at the ready. Making anticipations clearer means that the experiment is less threatening to the young person. They will be able to compare the results with their anticipations and then manage the outcome better, taking what Kelly called the Person as Scientist position. This is as an experimenter who tries something out, looks at the results and draws conclusions.

Therapy sessions might use techniques drawn from PCP or from other models, or new ones might arise within a therapeutic encounter. (The latter is how the first version of Drawing the Ideal Self came about.) There are no techniques that must be placed at a particular point in the process and some techniques may be repeated if that makes sense, or used for a different purpose. The great thing about PCP is that it is possible to use techniques drawn from other models of therapy. As long as the technique is used in order to understand the construing of the young person, it can be helpful. However, I find that PCP techniques are more useful. They will be designed to demonstrate personal construing and they are more likely to include elaborating the contrast poles as part of their process. You will find some examples in the Techniques section.

HOMEWORK

There is no requirement for homework but it can be useful. Remember that the primary place to experiment with construing is the therapy session because the implications need to be considered. However, there are times when you might want that experimentation to transfer to the outside world. This might be because you feel that the young person is ready to try something out and they will manage the outcomes. Try to work out what level of work outside sessions might be do-able for the young person you are working with, in their current circumstances. It is probably better to call it an experiment rather than homework, because young people will have constructs about school homework. If they already construe homework as difficult, or that it has to be perfect, or that it is stressful, calling work outside therapy sessions homework is unlikely to be helpful.

There are two alternatives that have been useful to me. An easy one is to suggest mulling something over until our next session (which means paying attention to construing and thinking about it) or noticing something. For example, "Have a think about why teachers might become so 'bad-tempered' with you when you call out in class." "See how many times your teacher shouts at you in the lesson this week."

Alternatively, you might offer the possibility of the young person doing an experiment outside your session that could tell them something interesting and allow them to opt in. It is important to make this a very open discussion so they can consider what they might do. They will need to be warned of the danger of over-committing in terms of the effort experiments can take - one thing is usually enough. Stress that you will be interested to talk about how it went and what they found out, but if they don't do it, you will not be telling them off (again, avoiding being like school homework). It is important that the responsibility for suggested experiments lies with the therapist and you will need to experiment with how, when and what sort of experiments will be completed. Attending therapy sessions is actually a big piece of work for a young person, requiring disruption to their usual routines. For some, this is more than enough without adding extra tasks. For others, they do not have the skills or support to work on things outside sessions.

An experiment can be anything that is related to your developing construction of the problem. For example, I worked with a young person around her anxiety about going out of the house and being around people. This meant that she had not attended school for the past two years and stayed in the house except when her parents took her out. The issue was associated with a strong desire to find her day absolutely predictable and she ran her days according to a detailed schedule. She told me that she had not changed her habits since she was five and that she had no wish to do so. That clearly was not the case but that was her construction of her life and of herself. My construing of her problem was that change was very threatening to her, so my invitation was around doing something (anything) that could show her that she already could (and did) make small changes *and* that changes could be temporary if they didn't suit her. We talked a lot about beginning things - finding a new TV programme, playing a new game, wearing different clothes, eating in a different seat - and drew attention to her theory not being as reliable as she had thought. I was curious to see whether she would tolerate trying other things and what they might be, so I invited her to do something (anything) she had not done before.

It began with a discussion about breakfast cereal. She said she had eaten the same cereal in exactly the same way and quantity for 10 years. My suggestion was met with horror when I suggested she might want to do an experiment with her breakfast - maybe eating two rather than three of the cereal biscuits with cold milk, or eating the usual three with warm milk, or perhaps putting fruit on it. She told me it was a stupid idea and that she didn't want to do it so we discussed what that might be about. That discussion made it clearer to me that her sense of herself as a person who never changed was a core construct. She realised that if she could change in one thing, she might become someone who made changes. This would mean that people might start to expect her to change other things. Then she might need to go to school again and to talk to people, her two biggest dreads. We discussed this at some length and I told her that she would not be returning to school at all, what ever happened. She was in Y11 and had not done any more than a very small number of GCSE courses provided through the home tuition service. The school would not be ready for her and she would not be ready to go into school before the exams, so it was ruled out. That was not something that had been understood by her before that session - she had assumed that my role was to get her back to school. She had never told anyone she thought that.

I invited her to experiment with a single change on one occasion only - not a change she had to stick with. We discussed all sorts of options and the cereal option was so far removed from going to school that it gradually became a viable option. I emphasised the role of experimenter because she was very interested in logic and science. She understood that the point was to do something different and evaluate the results. The evaluation would indicate whether to repeat the things in the experiment. She also understood that the experiment was to test her theory that she was unchanging. I explained that by attending her appointment, she had added something to her schedule, suggesting that some changes might be tolerable. She eventually agreed that if she felt like it, she might try something and come back and tell me.

To my surprise, she did do an experiment with the cereal and proved to herself that she was right about what to have for breakfast. My interest was in getting a cycle of experimentation going and this one experiment led to weekly experiments that gradually involved other people (saying good morning when she passed someone as she walked her dog). Our sessions were conducted using as much vocabulary from science and computing as I could because they were things she already understood well. Talking about theories (i.e. constructs), alternative possibilities and a testing process made sense to her. This was a young person who told me when the chairs in the room had moved from the previous week's positions and how they were different - she paid attention to details. We found a way to use our therapy sessions as a place to consider her personal constructs and how they arose, and to see what happened if they changed slightly. The homework was very helpful here because it provided more data for her to consider.

In some cases, it would be unwise ever to mention homework. This is particularly the case when the young person's experience of homework is associated with failure and getting into arguments at home and/or at school. Then, you might invite an experiment in an even more propositional way, suggesting that the experiment focusses on someone else's theory with something like this:

"It would be really interesting to know whether you are right about that teacher not treating you like everyone else. It could be true that he might not like you much and he would never help you. I wonder what would happen if, one day, you put your hand up rather than called him to you. Do you think you could get him to change? Could you get him to do something different?"

This is a much less direct challenge to face and can be an amusing way to get the child to do an experiment: "Could you get the teacher to change so much that he gives you a reward for that lesson? What if that happened? That would be such a shock to him!" In order to perform this experiment, the young person will be experimenting with their own construing but the attention is not focussed on their change. When this is evaluated, the young person's construing of themselves can also be discussed. This kind of experiment could be construed as a challenge. When we had a group for young people with eating problems and their parent, they each did a self-set challenge each week. The idea of their parent also doing a challenge was great fun for some of the young people. They loved the idea that they took the role of reminding the parent to do it. We wanted to introduce the idea of experimentation and review and that worked quite well.

When people do not do their experiments, that is interesting. If they have been carefully designed, properly agreed to and then do not happen despite the young person's intention to do them, you can be curious about why that is, but not critical. At these moments, I also remind myself of my own ability to change. It is often more difficult than I want it to be. I don't think I am alone in wanting to *have* changed rather than to *be changing*. I would love to skip right over to the new me! Luckily, PCP can be just as useful for exploring not doing something.

ENDING THERAPY

Ending therapy is a complicated thing. Sometimes it might be a little sad for you or the young person, especially when it has gone well. It is much more difficult to stop seeing someone who validates you as a therapist than it is to ending sessions with someone you feel you have failed with. It is also more comfortable to have a caseload made up of people you understand. The ending typically feels a bit too soon, whenever it happens. Perhaps this reflects a human desire to see something through to the end? However, PCP therapy sessions will only be getting people into a position so that they can continue the work through other people or through their own efforts. There is never a completely neat finishing position. You will not hear the end of the story unless someone gets in touch and tells you what happened after your sessions ended.

The other issue is that the young person should be able to develop a sense of agency and the role of the therapist should be more shaded. If the young person sees themselves as having done all the work and achieved all the gains, then that is exactly the result you might have hoped for. In my experience working with young people individually and in groups, the greatest gains often lead to the least acknowledgement of the role of therapy and my input to it.

This can be a bit disappointing for me as a person, because I would love to hear what a great job I did. As a therapist, I hope that this represents a more permanent change in the young person. I have worked in the same city for most of my life and I do occasionally come across people connected with the young people I have seen for therapy. I am really pleased when they tell me the rest of that young person or adult's story. Although it might be a biased sample, it is enough to keep me going in this profession!

It is important to remember that your final session may not be attended and to think about how you will handle this. Some people find endings painful and will avoid them. This could be as a non-attendance on the day, or as a cancellation. If they cancel, do you want to rearrange that ending session? You might do, if the session can be very soon and you are sure they will attend. You might not if your construing of the issue is that ending face-to-face will be difficult. When a colleague and I ran a PCP therapy group for adolescent girls who were depressed and self-harming, they so frequently missed their final session that we began to make sure we did a full review and said a proper goodbye on their penultimate session.

THE FINAL SESSION

There are some negotiations to be made with the client about who will receive what information about their therapy sessions and outcomes. The detailed content will need to be kept as private as possible but if you are trying to change the way people construe the young person through what you write, it will need more content. If you are working for a service, there will be rules about what can be shared and how. If you are working privately, the commissioner of your therapy time will probably want to know that it has happened and, in general, how it went. I will talk more about reporting your work in the next chapter.

In general, it can be helpful if the final session (or the final part of a single session consultation) also involves the person who came with the young person at the start. Sometimes, you might follow that by a meeting with a teacher if you want to enlist the school in supporting in a different way. If the work was commissioned by a school and took place there, you might have a conversation with the child and teacher at the end of the process. The discussions at the end are part of the therapeutic process: it is a sort of handover so that the parents or teacher (or both) can continue the work. Therapy sessions with you might be finished but the therapeutic processes of supporting reconstruing can continue. Formal therapy is a start but informal therapy will be occurring for some time to come.

If there have been a series of sessions, part of the final session would involve looking again at the starting point and any techniques used, and repeating them. This is part of having a clear round-up to the work. It is also very important to report the outcome measures in your report or letter about the work and to comment on them. Sometimes, significant change will not show on the measures you used at the start unless your measure is broad enough to capture real life changes. This is one reason we made Dimensions of Health and Well-being.

The final session will also need to include what will happen next and what to do if further problems arise. Generally, it is helpful to make the young person and parent/teacher aware that there might be a dip which makes them wonder whether the young person can manage without therapy sessions. This is about adjustment and should improve over time, if there is effective support to help the young person to maintain progress. It is not usually helpful to refer back to therapy immediately because part of your work will have aimed to encourage the young person to be more independent in addressing their difficulties. That means that the young person can be independent in seeking advice and support, not independent in managing it all. This aim means that you would need to work out a plan with the young person. If you can help the young person to anticipate that they might need some help and nominate a list of specific supporters (usually parents and teachers), you can add that information to your end of therapy letters.

TECHNIQUES

A START-UP TOOL BOX

I have separated out my explanations for a few key PCP techniques so that you can refer back to them more easily. If you learn to do these well, you will have enough to get you started with most cases. All these techniques can be used with a client of any age - they are just as useful for working with adults. The first three are PCP techniques that you will have to learn in order to be fluent in Personal Construct Therapy:

- How to find out what a person's constructs are (i.e. eliciting constructs).
- How to explore the detail of what a construct implies (i.e. pyramiding a construct). When laid out on paper, this looks like a pyramid.
- How to find out how a construct is connected to that person's most important (core) constructs (i.e. laddering a construct). When laid out on paper, this looks like a ladder.

Next there are four techniques that can be used for particular explorations in therapy. There are plenty of other techniques within the PCP world - this is simply a set to get you started. They represent my construing of therapy and they should be useful for common reasons for young people to be referred: their behaviour is not understood; they are struggling in relation to other people's expectations of them within a particular role (e.g. pupil); or they have had a difficult experience that changed them.

- How to explore a person's view of their own development and their personal ambitions (Drawing the Ideal Self).
- How to explore personal construing in relation to a small group using the Perceived Element Grid (PEG) (Procter, 1996).
- How to explore a person's construing of self in a role (Super Simple Role Rating).
- How to explore the impact of a difficult experience on a person's sense of self (Belgrade Difficult Experience Comic Strip Technique).

You can use all these techniques at no cost. You can also make variations for techniques, as long as you credit the original author and provide the reference to that work. This is the way techniques evolve and new developments add to the richness of PCP literature.

USING MATERIALS

The techniques I have designed usually involve some drawing. With both visual and verbal information, there is a much better possibility of understanding someone's construing. Often children and young people can express themselves more easily in drawing than in words. It gets away from the need to be precise, or to have a good vocabulary. The quality of drawing skill may be an issue but you can ask them to tell you what a drawing is, ideally that should be immediately after they finish (in case they cannot 'read' their own drawings later) but sometimes you can ask later in the process. If a person is an excellent artist, the drawings they produce may be much more informative than the words they use.

As children grow up, they may have come to construe themselves as 'unable to draw' or decided that they do not like to draw. Therefore, all my techniques ask for "a quick sketch" rather than a drawing. People who are good at drawing can make this as good as they like within the time available. People who are less comfortable can draw stick figures, shapes or scribbles. As long as they know what they have drawn, that will be fine. If someone refuses to draw, you can do your best to work through the technique with talking. The aim is to understand a person's construing - all techniques are a means to that end. You might either try a different technique or miss out the drawing parts, asking the person to describe or tell you rather than to draw.

To make the drawings good for scanning and copying black biros and white printer paper work well. Avoid a gel pen in case it smudges, and a pencil because they may not make a dark enough mark on the paper. Having coloured pens/pencils available might be great for an artist but selecting colours takes more time and will not necessarily show on a scanned copy.

If you do the writing parts of a task for a person, they are not limited by their spelling or writing abilities. If they insist on doing their own writing, it helps to emphasise that they can choose any words they want and not worry about the spelling.

Having a combination of drawing and writing makes it easier for both the therapist and the client to recall what the person said or did in the session. Each session can begin with a review of what was done, showing any material from the previous session. This helps both the therapist and client to 'tune in' to the session.

CAUTION

This book is aimed at people who have some knowledge of PCP already and will already have some form of professional training. That training will have emphasised the importance of professional behaviour and boundaries. It will also have informed the professional of their duties in terms of safeguarding children and adults. All PCP techniques can move quickly from something that seems to be not too important to illuminating big issues in a person's life. Therefore, it will be important to act within your role and not stray into territory that you may not be able to manage well within that role. It is assumed that if you are using this technique you are already qualified and working in a way which provides the necessary safety for your clients and yourself.

I have included the Belgrade Difficult Experiences Comic Strip Technique in this book. This may be be more useful to people offering therapy through health services or private work or but less useful for community-based professions such as educational psychology or speech and language therapy if they have a different focus and no possibility of working over a number of sessions. This is not related to a profession but to the role the therapist is commissioned to fulfil. For example, a speech and language therapist working therapeutically with people who have had a head injury might find it extremely useful. An educational psychologist working with a child who has been avoiding school since they moved to a secondary school might find that this technique clarifies why it was so distressing. The impact of any experience is related to that individual's construing. Therefore, it may be very appropriate for professionals working in a community setting to address difficult experiences around bullying, bereavement and loss, or a big change of culture (e.g. moving house, moving country or going to a different kind of school).

Your work may illuminate a more severe impact on mental health (e.g. symptoms of PTSD, depression), or an issue which you anticipate will require longer term therapy (e.g. abuse, exploitation, domestic abuse). If it is not appropriate to your role to address these or you will not be able to commit longer term work, you will need to discuss referring the young person to a more appropriate service.

Working with a very difficult experience that has traumatised a young person presents the possibility of re-traumatising the young person and of the therapist being traumatised by the material. These are issues to be considered and discussed carefully in supervision before starting the work.

Offering therapy sessions needs to be well organised and within a safe space (i.e. location, time and without unplanned interruption to a session or to a series of sessions). This will be important for contracting sessions if they are school-based because it is not the usual business of schools. The staff there may not be aware of the importance of the conditions around the work you are doing so make your requirements very clear.

1. HOW TO FIND OUT WHAT A PERSON'S CONSTRUCTS ARE (ELICITING CONSTRUCTS)

A construct is *bipolar* - it has two ends (e.g. Happy vs. Sad). It is also *dimensional*, with the possibility of being more or less of whatever it is. The whole construct will only be clear when you have both poles of the construct. This is because the contrast pole could be anything. The two ends are called the emergent pole and the contrast pole.

The *emergent pole* of a construct is the end of the construct that the client presents to you in the conversation with you or in an exercise like a grid (i.e. it emerges).

The *contrast pole* is the end of the construct you will have to ask for and only becomes clear in relation to the emergent pole because it is used in contrast to that pole.

STEP 1: FIND THE CONSTRUCTS

You can find the emergent pole of a construct very easily, just by listening (or reading) to what a person says. The constructs are underlined in Emily's discussion about her teachers.

"I think that teachers are <u>rude</u> - but they get away with it. They don't <u>use their manners</u> when they speak to kids but they expect us to always use ours, even when they have just been rude to us. My maths teacher is <u>alright</u> - she is better than the rest - but only when she is <u>in a good mood</u>. Since I have been here, the <u>best teachers</u> have always left to get a better job - because this school is <u>a bad school</u>. The ones we are left with can't even teach a class without <u>boring us to death</u>. They make use do so much work and there is never any time for <u>a little chat or a joke with them</u>."

STEP 2: FIND THE CONTRAST POLES

You can do this by asking something like, "How would you describe someone who isn't X?" Or "What is the contrast to X?" Or "If the person isn't X, what would they be like?" Try to avoid the client using the word 'opposite' so that they do not give you a dictionary definition. Constructs are usually written with a hyphen between the poles (happy-sad) or using versus (vs.) (happy vs. sad). I think it helps to write them down - unless you have a great memory!

Rude vs. Polite

Use their manners vs. speak to kids as dirt

Alright vs. terrible

Good mood vs. Bad mood

Bad school vs. Top school

Best teachers vs. Worst teachers

Boring us to death vs. Making the lesson fun

A little chat or a joke with them vs. Too serious and strict.

STEP 3: CHECK OUT SIMILAR USE OF WORDS

Bear in mind that you may find that two (or more) seem to be the same construct. For example:

Lazy vs. Hardworking

Tries hard vs. Does not make an effort.

Alternatively, constructs with a similar verbal label (on either the emergent or contrast pole) might turn out to be very different from each other. For example:

Smart vs. Stupid

Cool dresser vs. Smart

The way to check out whether they are similar or different is to ask more about their meaning, perhaps through pyramiding (see the next section).

2. HOW TO EXPLORE THE DETAIL OF A CONSTRUCT (PYRAMIDING)

WHAT IS IT?

Pyramiding is finding about the details of a construct. Technically, it involves moving from a construct that has many implications because it is more abstract (e.g. teacher) to more specific constructs (e.g. stands at the front, tells me to get my work done, shows me how to add numbers, reads stories to me). I think of it as moving down the construct system, away from core constructs towards towards something that might be observable (i.e. towards peripheral constructs). This is useful because peripheral constructs are usually easier to reconstrue - they are less important to the person so changing them is less threatening.

WHEN IS IT USEFUL?

Pyramiding is really useful for finding details about construing that could help you to find something definite to work with. In Emily's case, you would want to find out exactly what she meant by some of the constructs she used, for example, finding out more about "A little chat or a joke with them" vs. "Too serious and strict".

Pyramiding can be used conversationally or by drawing it out in a diagram. Remember that unless you ask for the contrast pole, you do not know what the construct is and you will not be clear what the young person is talking about. As you move down a pyramid, you will find more concrete detail.

HOW TO DO IT

I would usually ask something like, "If I watched a video of X, what would that be like - what would I see and hear?"; "How would you know if someone was X - what would they be doing?"

This example is pyramiding one of Emily's constructs. Read this pyramid from the top downwards. This reveals some details that could be important for indicating how to help Emily have a better start to her lesson.

If I tried to help Emily to have a better start to her lessons, I would want to enlist her teacher's help. I would ask her to smile at Emily at the start of every lesson and give her a minute to choose a seat herself so that Emily is more likely to construe the teacher as friendly. I might also propose that the teacher takes an informal, jokey approach if she has to ask Emily to stop doing something. I would also let her teacher know how important the games and quizzes are to Emily. She wants to be engaged with the teacher and talk about her own interests so the teacher might find out a bit more about her and have a short reference to her football matches as part of her welcoming Emily to the class.

Another possibility would be to discuss Emily doing an experiment with her own construing. She might try sitting down quickly and smiling at the teacher when she enters the room and report the results of her experiments back to me. This could change the teacher's anticipation of Emily and lead to a different response from the teacher. From my own experience, I would suggest that the strategy of helping the teacher to understand Emily better is likely to have greater success because her teacher's construing of her might lead to an unhelpful response (e.g. sarcasm, public surprise) rather than something validating for Emily. It is very difficult for all of us to understand and accept changes in other people and the teacher's anticipations of Emily (and her behaviour and intentions) will probably be hard to shift.

PYRAMID OF ONE OF EMILY'S CONSTRUCTS

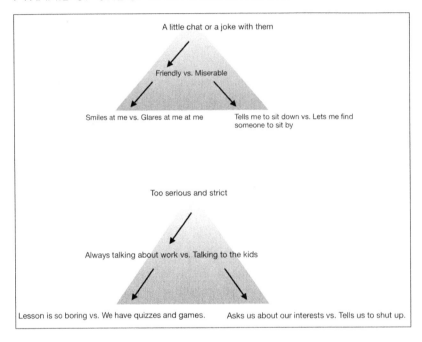

3. HOW TO FIND OUT HOW A CONSTRUCT IS CONNECTED TO THAT PERSON'S MOST IMPORTANT (CORE) CONSTRUCTS (LADDERING A CONSTRUCT)

WHAT IS IT?

L addering is a process. I think of laddering as moving up through the construct system - climbing up the ladder from less important and more specific constructs towards more important and more abstract core constructs.

WHEN IS IT USEFUL?

It is a great way to find out about core constructs. Note that there is a caution about laddering - it looks easier than it is and it really needs practice. Once you have mastered it, it can be done in conversational style but it helps to write the constructs on the ladder where the client can see it. If not, you and they are liable to forget exactly what they said.

What you want to find out is how something that might be less important is linked to core construing. This will help you to work out what really matters to them.

HOW TO DO IT

You will start with a construct and if you only have the emergent pole it is crucial that you ask for the contrast pole. Check which pole (end) of the construct the client prefers then you need to find out why they prefer it. This is a step up the ladder towards core construing. Then go through the same questions for this construct - "Which do you prefer, X or Y". For each step up a ladder, you will need to ask something like, "Why is that important to you?" or "Why does that matter?"

At each step, be prepared that you might switch sides of the ladder - one side is no better than the other. The sides will relate to the emergent pole of a construct being expressed. There is no expectation that the preferred poles will all line up neatly on one side.

Remember that the intention is to have a conversation and to understand - getting it neatly on paper is secondary to that. This is why you cannot have a pro forma for laddering - you will never know how many rungs there will be. Writing it from the bottom to the top of the page might remind you that the ladder is moving from peripheral to core construing. Some people might prefer to work down the page. It does not matter, as long as you are consistent and remember that you are moving towards core construing.

You will know that you are reaching the top of the ladder because people find it harder to find the words to express their views. The client might take longer to think, shrug their shoulders and say they are not sure why it matters, or say something like "Because it does/is". Our core construing is not always put easily into words. You will notice that the constructs gradually become more about the meaning of life and less about specifics.

A LADDER USING ONE OF EMILY'S CONSTRUCTS

Read this ladder from the bottom of the page to the top - you will see that those at the top are core constructs.

If you don't have a home you won't be able to do anything	———	Have a family, be warm, go to work - having no home is a something that matters to everyone
People who don't pass exams might become homeless	———	Learning stuff helps kids to have a better life because they will get more pay
Teachers who don't care shouldn't be teachers	———	They are trying to help
Other people aren't trained to teach	———	Teachers are important to kids
It shows that the teacher doesn't care.	———	It shows that the teacher thinks about us and what we like.
Boring us to death	———	Making the lesson fun

4. HOW TO EXPLORE A PERSON'S VIEW OF THEIR OWN DEVELOPMENT AND THEIR PERSONAL AMBITIONS (DRAWING THE IDEAL SELF)

WHAT IS IT?

Drawing the Ideal Self is a version of a Self Characterisation that explores a person's construing of self. It includes a rating of self esteem, a view of past and potential future personal growth and this leads into personal goal setting. It also invites suggestions for supporting future development.

WHEN IS IT USEFUL?

This technique is really useful in the initial phase of therapy but it can be used in any phase. It can be completed with a person of any age but it was originally designed to use with a child or young person. It is particularly helpful when other people feel they do not understand how a young person might behave in the ways they do.

HOW TO DO IT

Detailed instructions for this technique are available in the free manual **Drawing the Ideal Self: A Personal Construct Technique to**

Explore Self Esteem. It includes an example and how to report its use. The manual can be downloaded from my website as a complete booklet. You will also find an instruction sheet to take into a session: drawingtheidealself.co.uk.

There is a copy of information in the manual in the Resources section but you might also want to download from the website it as a separate booklet because its illustrations are larger.

5. HOW TO EXPLORE PERSONAL CONSTRUING IN RELATION TO A SMALL GROUP (PERCEIVER ELEMENT GRID - PEG)

WHAT IS IT?

The Perceiver Element Grid (PEG) (Procter, 1996) is a lovely, easy to use grid which invites the client to consider how people construe each other. It can be analysed immediately, within the session. Harry Procter is the designer and you can learn about it from Harry himself by reading his original paper:

https://www.academia.edu/1810615/The_Family_Construct_System_1996_

or watch Harry explaining the technique on You Tube:

https://youtu.be/z3uS7UA0P9M.

WHEN IS IT USEFUL?

The PEG is great for asking a young person about how they think individuals in a group construe each other. That might be a family, a group of friends, or any other sort of small group or team. I have also used it to consider a young person's views of a group of their teachers. The young person will be using their own construing so you will learn a lot about how they make sense of other people, and therefore, the constructs they might apply to themselves. When you eyeball the PEG, you will notice repeating constructions - the young person using the same or similar language to construe a number of people. This indicates that these might be more important constructs to that individual.

The PEG can be also completed 'live' in a group, by the group members rather than by one person doing the whole grid. Harry used the PEG in family therapy sessions. It can also be completed in separate parts by the group members each doing their row. The rows can be compiled into the grid and shared in a meeting with the group for an interesting discussion.

HOW TO DO IT

The young person will be asked something like, "How do you think X sees Y?" or "What does X think of Y?" Asking for three descriptors for each person, makes the picture richer. Remember that the descriptor you will be given is the emergent pole of a construct and unless you ask for the contrast pole afterwards you will not know what the construct is.

When you are eliciting the constructs for each person, you work across the rows, rather than down the columns. You will see that *Me* is last on each list, so that the flow of the process is established before you ask more directly for their personal construing.

Have a look at the completed grid and consider what is a repeating construct or a similar construct. The repeating ones are likely to be more important constructs. If you take the repeating ones, you could then ask for the contrast poles. Once you have that construct, you can make a rating along the construct, placing all the people in the family along the continuum. If you do that, it is helpful to ask for a rating of *self* and *ideal self* so that you can see whether there is a difference.

A COMPLETED PEG

Have a look at the PEG below and see what constructs you might want to explore further.

	Mum	Dad	Sister	Me
Mum	Stressed at times Busy Loves her kids	Strict Funny Loves running	Moans a lot A teenager Wants her own way all the time	Funny Lazy Hates school
Dad	Soft Easy going Nice	Likes to win Friendly Very funny	Very irritating at times Kind sometimes Wants her own way too much	Lazy A joker Good at rugby
Sister	Funny Strict Bossy	Too strict Thinks he is funny Always late	Intelligent Arty Not good looking	Annoying A baby Can be funny
Me	Bossy Funny Likes sports	Can have a good laugh Likes sports Too strict about homework	Can be nice when she is in a good mood Too bossy to me Thinks she is the centre of the universe	Likes a joke Lazy at school Good at rugby

Reference

Procter, H.G. (1996). The Family Construct System. In Kalekin-Fishman, D. & Walker, B. (Eds) The Structure of Group Realities: Culture and Society in the Light of Personal Construct Theory. Malabar, Florida: Krieger.

6. HOW TO EXPLORE A PERSON'S CONSTRUING OF SELF IN A ROLE (SUPER SIMPLE ROLE RATING)

WHAT IS IT?

The Super Simple Role Rating is an easy way to work through a detailed look at a role a person plays. This could be a role they have chosen (e.g. musician) or been assigned (e.g. student). The technique takes you through a loosening and tightening cycle, and ends with generating potential actions.

WHEN IS IT USEFUL?

This technique is suitable for use in therapy and in coaching and personal development. It can be used to explore any kind of role - e.g. teacher, student, parent, son/daughter, friend. PCP is based on understanding an individual person's construing and makes no judgement about whether that is socially acceptable. Therefore, this technique can also be used to explore roles that would be seen as problematic by society - e.g. gang member, thief, abuser, self-harmer. It is particularly useful when it is difficult to understand a person's construing of a particular role and how their actions might make sense to them.

It can be used with adults and children so it can be equally useful to work through with a parent or a person moving into a new role (e.g. a newly qualified teacher). Some people might be very reluctant to draw the sketches used as part of this technique. If they cannot be encouraged to draw, then you can ask for a description instead. The technique will still work but the drawings are part of the loosening process and I would be reluctant to miss them out.

HOW TO DO IT

Follow the instructions below. There is an illustrated booklet for this technique that is freely available on my website. This will be easier to take into a session as a reminder of the process. Download the PDF from drawingtheidealself.co.uk.

～

THE SUPER SIMPLE ROLE RATING

All of us will have a number of roles to play in life (e.g. daughter, parent, grandchild, accountant, tennis player, patient, therapist, teacher, student). This technique can be used to explore any role.

It involves three parts: eliciting constructs, selecting the more important ones and then completing a rating scale. I have broken it down into a lot of steps to make it clearer but it is not difficult to do. Remember not to get drawn into discussion at the earlier stages of this technique otherwise the task will be hard to complete quickly. It will probably take 60-90 minutes if you follow these instructions and it could be completed across a couple of sessions (with a break before Part 3).

Make sure that you test it out on yourself before you use it with someone else so that you are clear about what to do at each step.

～

Equipment

A4 paper x 5 (with a couple spare in case you need more space)
  Black pen

Process

Part 1 (Steps 1&2) - eliciting constructs and finding contrast poles
  Part 2 (Steps 3&4) - selecting the constructs for the grid
  Part 3 (Steps 7-9) - completing construct ratings and generating experiments to move towards the ideal on each construct.

Step 1 - Elicit the first set of emergent poles of constructs - the 8 worst XX

Paper 1 in landscape orientation.
  Divide it into 8, giving you 8 boxes to draw in.
  Ask the client to make a quick sketch of the **8 <u>worst</u> XX they can imagine** (where XX is the role you want to explore e.g. footballer), drawing one in each box.
  When you have them all, ask the client to name each one in a way that characterises them: "Give each one a name that tells us what s/he is like." This is the emergent pole of the construct.

Step 2 - Elicit the second set of emergent poles of constructs - the 8 best XX

Paper 2 in landscape orientation.
  Divide it into 8, giving you 8 boxes to draw in.
  Ask the client to make a quick sketch of the **8 <u>best</u> XX they can imagine** (where XX is the same role from Step 1), drawing one in each box.

When you have them all, ask them to name each one in a way that characterises them. "Give each one a name that tells us what s/he is like."

This is another set of emergent poles.

You now have two sets of 8 sketches. Lay them out, side-by-side allow you both to see all 16 pictures and to make the next step easier.

Step 3 - List the emergent poles of the 16 constructs

Paper 3 in portrait orientation.

On the left side of the paper, list the emergent poles of your 16 constructs from Steps 1 & 2 - the order does not matter but make sure you don't miss any.

Emergent pole vs.

E.g.

Ball hogger vs.

Team player vs.

Step 4 - Find the contrast poles for each of the 16 constructs

Ask for the contrast pole for each construct and write it on the right hand side - e.g. ask "How would you describe someone who is NOT XX ?" (where XX is the emergent pole).

Emergent pole vs. contrast pole

E.g.

Ball hogger vs. Good passer

Team player vs. Selfish player

Step 5 - Find the preferred pole of each construct

Circle the preferred end of each construct. Avoid the temptation to merge Steps 6 and 7 time because their selection may be different once they can see all of the constructs with both poles.

∾

Step 6 - Choose the 6 most important constructs

Ask the client to choose the **six constructs** that matter most to the them. If they really need to have a couple more or fewer, that is fine - it will just take more or less time to complete the rest of the task. Asking for at least six means that they need to make some choices between constructs so you will get the more meaningful ones.

∾

Step 7 - Rating preparation

Paper 4 & 5 in landscape orientation. Using your 6 constructs, write the non-preferred pole on the left hand side of the page. To give you plenty of room to work through the rest of the task, it will be easier if you have 3 constructs on paper 4 and then 3 on paper 5. Draw a line to the other side and add the other pole from your list.

∾

Step 8 - Complete by rating one construct at a time

To do this part of the technique means working methodically through each construct.

Take one construct at a time, repeating this process.

Ask the client to mark **self now, self on my worst ever day** and **ideal self**, self at a couple of relevant other time points (e.g. me when I move to a better team, me when I am an adult, me next year).

～

Step 9 - Generate experiments

Draw an arrow between **now** and **ideal** to illustrate the distance between the two and to show the direction of movement. What could be done to help them to move closer to their ideal? Ask for 2 ideas for each construct - something the client can start doing tomorrow and something others could do. If the client wants to give you more than 2 suggestions, that is even better. These are potential ways forward for the client but you might also want to seek consent to let other people know about how they might offer effective support. If help and encouragement comes in a way that makes sense to the client, it is more likely to be construed as helpful.

～

Note about the number of pictures

If you work with someone who finds it too difficult to think of eight examples, you can reduce the number. Sometimes, that could be about not being able to visualise something to draw, or about not having enough constructs in relation to the role to provide eight. This might also apply if you are working with someone very young, or if they struggle to construe people and psychological characteristics, such as in autism. However, it is important never to make assumptions about the ability to construe so I would not recommend limiting how many you ask for before the session. You will be using all the constructs in the end (those on the **worst** *and* **best** lists) but the fewer you have, the less chance there is of you finding out what is important to that individual. As you go through the process, you can decide to reduce the number according to the response of that individual. You might want to offer the option to tell you rather than to draw, but I would encourage drawing because it will mean using other constructs, not only those that are easily translated into words.

It is worth looking closely at the drawings because you will not know the significance of what is drawn and there might be something important to notice.

7. HOW TO EXPLORE THE IMPACT OF A DIFFICULT EXPERIENCE ON A PERSON'S SENSE OF SELF (BELGRADE DIFFICULT EXPERIENCE COMIC STRIP TECHNIQUE)

WHAT IS IT?

The Belgrade Difficult Experience Comic Strip Technique is a way to explore how an experience has affected someone's construing of themselves and of their potential future ideal self. Its name comes from a workshop in Belgrade's PCP psychotherapy school where I described the technique and showed how it worked. Until that day it had no name but I realised that it needed one so that other people might be able to try it.

WHEN IS IT USEFUL?

This technique can be used after a young person has struggled with the impact of a difficult experience, often where concerned others have reported a significant change in them since the event/s. Personal Construct Theory makes it clear that there are no universal interpretations of any experience and that the implications of the same experience will be personal to each individual. Therefore, the impact of a difficult experience is related to the interpretation and implications rather than some sort of quantifiable event. This is what

PCP is all about - the personal construing of experiences. The Belgrade Difficult Experience Comic Strip can be used at any point in therapy and if you have already completed the Drawing the Ideal Self technique, there is no need to redo it. There are three components:

1. Drawing the Ideal Self;
2. The creation of a comic strip telling the story of the difficult experience;
3. Discussion and exploration of the implications of the first two parts.

HOW TO DO IT

Follow the instructions below. There is an illustrated booklet for this technique that is freely available on my website. This will be easier to take into a session as a reminder of the process. Download the PDF from drawingtheidealself.co.uk.

THE BELGRADE DIFFICULT EXPERIENCE COMIC STRIP TECHNIQUE

This technique follows a process for exploring a difficult or traumatic experience. It will take *at least* two sessions to work through the two first parts of the technique and then further session/s to consider and discuss the findings and the implications.

Equipment

A4 paper (at least 8 sheets - 3 for Drawing the Ideal Self, the rest for the difficult experience comic strip)
    Black pen

~

Process summary

Part 1 is completing Drawing the Ideal Self
  Part 2 is completing the difficult experience comic strip
  Part 3 is discussing the implications of the difficult experience.

~

Step 1 - Complete Drawing the Ideal Self

This is important so that you can get to know the client and the way he/she wants to develop before you explore the difficult experience. This way, when you explore that experience, you may be able to understand better why it affected the person as it did. The instructions are included in the Resources section and are freely download-able from www.drawingtheidealself.co.uk. There is a manual and a prompt sheet to take into a session and remind you of the process. Please read manual first, rather than relying only on the prompt sheet.

~

Step 2 - Difficult experience comic strip

Take an A4 paper and divide it into 8 rectangles (tearing or cutting the paper so there are separate rectangles). You are likely to need more than one set of 8 so have spare paper to make more rectangles as needed. Use them so that all the drawings are all in the same orientation (otherwise your comic strip will be messy).

Ask the client to think about the difficult experience and draw pictures for every part of their story that they can remember. This will include the lead up, the experience itself and the aftermath. The story will emerge gradually and you will not know where in the story the client will start their comic strip. This is why the pictures are on separate pieces of paper. They might add information and details into the story at a later point, when something occurs to them. I have often found that when the story makes a more coherent whole, and the person looks at it in a comic strip format, more recollections and details emerge. These are easily added into the comic strip by inserting a new drawing.

Ask something like:

"Can you draw a picture on these small bits of paper for each part of your story? We will make the whole story piece by piece and you don't have to remember it in order because we can add pictures or move them around as you want. What's the first thing you can remember about it?"

Once that is done, you can move backwards and forwards from that picture: "What happened next?" "What was happening before that?" "Did anything happen between these two pictures?" The order of the drawings will be determined by the client, so what you will find is the sense they made of what happened. This may not match the descriptions provided by reports from other people but that does not matter because this is their personal construction of events.

Once the client is comfortable with their account, you can fix the comic parts in their order. The easiest way is to glue them onto another A4 sheet in groups of 8. At that point, you can number them, if that helps. Then take a photo or make a scanned copy of the whole story.

Ask the client to show you the worst three parts of what happened and mark them with an asterisk or some similar mark. From these three, ask them to identify the very worst part for them and mark the picture with two asterisks or a star.

~

Step 3 - Implications of the difficult experience

From your knowledge of your client's Drawing the Ideal Self, consider how the difficult experience might have impacted on their sense of self. Discuss how they think the experience might have affected them. E.g. Did it interfere with their progress towards their ideal self? Did they get stuck somehow because of it? What important things did they learn about themselves or others, or life itself, through having this difficult experience? Has anything useful come out of it?

To start this discussion, you can add some additional ratings to Drawing the Ideal Self rating scale. The following may be helpful but you may think of others that are related to the client's story:

Where would you put yourself on this scale before [difficult experience] happened?

Where were you after it happened?

Where would your parents have put you on on this scale before [difficult experience] happened?

What about afterwards?

Where do you think you might have been now on this scale if that hadn't happened to you?

Look at the parts of their story that they identified as the worst parts and discuss why they were the worst. You will find that there are constructs to explore in more detail. There is very likely to be a link between the experience of distress and core construing (e.g. "I thought I was going to die!" "I thought I would never see my mum again!" "I wanted to run home and the teacher said I had to wait to be picked up!").

Discuss why the experience might have been so difficult in relation what you know of the client's construing. This might help them to understand why the experience was so difficult. This should be done tentatively, trying out possible connections in a way that the client can refute. (e.g. "I wonder if there is a connection between your views that family is really important and supports you, and the possibility that your mum could die?") The discussion should enable the client to see connections so they can make sense of why their experience was difficult for them.

The final part of the work is to consider what useful aspects of the experience there might be. This could be anything e.g. they learned to cross roads more carefully; they realised that they could live on after their mum died but that they should always remember that people do die; they knew that they could survive an awful thing and still pass school exams. The idea is to pay attention to the future and to consider that there are alternative ways to construe themselves and the difficult experience.

This is also a point where the therapist can offer reflections on what they have noticed through the facilitation of the technique. The therapist can also go back to Drawing the Ideal Self and ask the client where they think they might be in a year's time on the rating scale. This will provide an indication of whether they can see that they anticipate that they will grow and move towards their ideal despite this difficult experience. It is helpful to explore what the factors might contribute to this anticipated move up or down the rating scale. Then there can be a discussion about what they or other people could do to support their development.

If they anticipate a decline in their development (i.e. movement towards the kind of person they do not want to be like) then the focus would be on trying to be clear about why and how they expect that to happen and who or what could minimise the decline. This would also mean looking for exceptions so that the sort of decline becomes clearer, rather than it being a generalised decline.

A note about asking for drawings

If you work with someone who finds it difficult to make drawings, you might wish to invite a description instead. I suggest that you wait until you know that they are struggling with drawing part of the task, rather than offering it as an option at the beginning. If your client cannot be encouraged to draw, don't worry about that because you can write the description for them and use the same comic strip approach. It will be more difficult to 'view' the whole comic strip so it might help to give each one a short title related to what happened. Remember that you are trying to get the whole story down so do not get focussed on finding every detail otherwise you will not be able to reach that point.

WRITING ABOUT
YOUR WORK

CONSIDER THE IMPLICATIONS
BEFORE YOU WRITE

The first decision to make with writing is the format you will need to use for this individual situation. In my opinion, reports are more formal and less personalised and stand as a record of what was done and any recommendations. A letter has the advantage that it is written to a person, rather than about them. This means that the letter can be adjusted to *your* construing of *the audience's* construing of the young person's involvement in therapy. In therapy, the most likely audiences are young person, parents, teacher/social worker, and other professionals. There are no neutral letters (or reports) - all will involve your construing of the referral, the problem/s, and the therapy. If your writing only serves as an information record, then it will miss an opportunity to help the young person to understand what happened and for the parents/teachers/professionals to offer more effective support.

What will your letter do?

If you tailor your letter to include therapeutic messages, then it is part of the therapy. It can serve as a reminder of your discussions but also of the alternative constructions that have lead to progress.

Change is difficult and maintaining change is harder so the letter can also include encouragement for times when it is more of a challenge.

Before you write and send any letter, it is important to consider the implications for the child, parents and teacher. In the UK, services will usually require therapists to keep a record of their work and to make a summary at the end of it. This is often shared with the referrer. Note that the referral was only made as a result of discussion with a concerned parent or professional - the referrer provided a gateway. What they will want to know is more straightforward: was the referral appropriate; was therapy effective; and are there things they need to do as a result of your therapy finishing. This will be found within your letter but it will take time to read through so you might want to write a separate very short covering letter, especially if the referrer was a GP or paediatrician.

Remember that your letter may not be used only for *your* intended purpose. You may write it as a summary of what you have done in order to remind the child, their parents and teacher but it could be used later in an application for resources (e.g. in the education special needs system or be included with a referral to another service). The child's parents or teacher may decide to share it with other people, particularly other professionals, so it will need to be written in way that is understandable without much knowledge of the context.

Whom will you write to?

The letter, in any format, forms part of the therapeutic intervention. The first possible recipient of your letter is the young person. This means using simpler language, incorporating useful diagrams, and including messages to encourage the young person in the future. You can talk to the young person about the possible future use of the letter and ask about what they might want it to do for them. If the young person is old enough and sensible enough to deny the letter going to anyone else (or does not want to have any letter from you) it still will be important to write something to the referrer. This can be the essential information only and include the fact that the young person has opted for their information to remain confidential so it cannot be shared. I would recommend having a serious discussion with the young person about the value of letting parents and professionals know about the important parts of the therapeutic encounter. In my view, there is a great deal to be gained by sharing, if you can do it well. Even when the young person does not want a letter about their therapy, it will still be useful to send something as closure of their relationship with you. It might be short but it can include a goodbye message and a reminder that the path to progress is not easy.

Your letter might be sent directly to the young person, rather than being included with the parent's copy. This emphasises the separateness of the relationship with you and means that they can read it before their parent reads it. I would always send a copy to the parent as well because young people will not necessarily look after it and it could be needed in the future.

The second option is to write it to the parents/teacher/social worker - whomever is the instigator of the referral. With this option, you will need to have discussed their concerns with them so that you can write in a way that fits with their construing. The letter should not be an invalidating experience for the reader so you will need to take care with presenting alternative constructions from those the parents/teacher has of the young person. You will want them to read the whole thing, not get to the point where they are uncomfortable and give up.

When will you write it?

Another consideration is when the letter is written. It will be important to provide information but do not break your confidentiality agreement with the parent or young person. Therefore, you might write it and share it with the young person before the end of therapy. I would usually read it aloud to them so that I can add the tone to the words. Sharing the letter at this point means you have a chance to see their reaction to it and to make any agreed changes before the end of the work.

Alternatively, a letter might be written by the young person to the adults involved. In some cases, I have used videos of the young person explaining what will help them as and additional part of the reporting. This might run into headaches with data protection and consent so it is vital that the permission of the young person and their parents is given freely and that the video is theirs to share with whomever they wish. The letter or report would refer to the video being available to watch via the child and parents.

In some cases, what you write could pose some difficulty for other people unless you are very careful with your use of language and phrasing. For example, if the child has talked a lot about their teacher and how the teacher's style and manner leads to them feeling worse, this will need to be reported very sensitively and in a way that does not invalidate that teacher. The same would apply if the relationship with their parent has been a focus in the work. However, your letter could help an adult to understand that young person better and this means that they may be able to offer better help to them in future. If that is the aim, you will have to write with that in mind and consider the language and tone to use so that their reconstruction might be facilitated.

There are some examples of letters in the next sections which give a flavour of how they might be written - but these are only my own ideas. I have included them because I have never seen a book with such material in them and they could prove useful to someone.

EXAMPLE LETTER TO A YOUNG PERSON

Dear Billy,
  You will remember that you came to see me because your parents were really worried about your temper. When we met with your mum and dad, they explained how it affected the family and what happened when you 'lost it'. I was impressed by your maturity in joining in that discussion - it showed how serious you were about getting some help.

We started with a session with you and your parents and we talked about the way you have developed over your childhood. Then you and I met for four sessions. I also met with your mum on her own to talk about some of the issues you brought up. Our last session was with your mum and you.

We used a number of different tools and techniques to help you to tell me about your own views. Your parents had explained that you always were 'fiery', even as a toddler, but as you grew up your temper seemed to get out of hand too often. You told me that you did not mean to get so angry but that it happened so quickly you couldn't seem to stop it. Your parents knew it was hard for you to keep yourself calm at home and they thought I might be able to help you to control it better. I had a letter from your teacher which we discussed and she said that you seemed to control yourself pretty well in school, even when you fell out with your friends. Your teacher also talked about how you have been a star in the school musicals and in the rugby team.

This difference between you at home and school was interesting. In our sessions together we looked at the way you saw things and you were great at explaining your views. We used a technique to help you to explain about your two versions of yourself - Home Billy and School Billy. You could tell me what the two versions of Billy did when they were faced with a challenge that could make them angry. You told me about the strategies you try in school, like walking off, or going to the toilet, or shouting to yourself. They work pretty well. At home, you have found it really hard to find some good strategies so you have ended up screaming, crying and slamming the doors. Sometimes you have sworn at people. Sometimes, you have hit your brother and sister and once you threatened to hit your mum. This was a really difficult thing to talk about because you know that you don't want to hit your mum at all and you were scared you that you could. Your mum had the same fear but she knew that you care a lot about her and that was not how you wanted to behave.

We had a good discussion about your brother and sister and you. You explained that you are not happy with how you do at school compared to them. You thought that they were pretty clever and did things easily and that you had to try really hard to learn in school. You also thought that your sister and brother thought you were 'dumb' because of this and when they teased you in an argument, you would feel dumb because you couldn't think what to say next. That meant that you were left with fighting back in a physical way because it was the only way to get your point across.

Interestingly, you seemed to not to be recognising that there are other areas of life where you did much better than lots of other people. You play rugby for the school and the county. You had to get selected for these squads and you have not missed being selected for a game yet. When you are on the pitch, you feel great and you work really hard. You have been Man of the Match and Players Player a few times, suggesting that the other team members recognise your achievements.

You are also learning the electric guitar and got your grade 3 recently. This wasn't easy because you have had to work hard on your exam pieces. You think you might be starting a band with two of your friends soon and your parents can see that you are *really* good at music. They like to hear you play and sing and you really enjoy rock music, like your dad.

One of the things we looked at is what a fiery temper is and how that ability to get angry easily might be useful at times. We will always need some people who get fired up quickly so that they can act immediately, when other people are still thinking about it. The tricky thing is to hold on to your temper when you are provoked. The only way to do that is to recognise it in yourself as something you will watch carefully. You were already doing that in school. You are starting to find ways to keep it under control at home too. From what you said, you are aware that it is not the anger that causes other people to get upset with you - it is what you do with your angry feelings. It sounds like you are developing your skills in controlling your hitting now. I know from what you said that you are still shouting and slamming doors sometimes. However, talking to your mum, she has seen a change in you. She has noticed that you have a different look on your face when you are angry and that you are shouting back at your brother and sister instead of hitting them. Your mum has spoken to them about your concerns and they are trying harder too. You told me that you have noticed a difference in them so they haven't irritated you so much lately.

In our sessions you have worked some things out which seem to have helped you. You want a career in sport or music and you do not need to be great at all your school work for these careers. You are also already good at the things you need so you have a good basis for development. We did a Drawing the Ideal Self exercise to look at what you did want and you have a clear view of yourself as a rugby player, and doing music as a way to earn extra money. You also want to be a sociable and friendly person at home and school. Your ideal family time is something you already do - going to watch the rugby match on Saturday and having dinner in a pub afterwards. The thing you would fear the most would be being lonely and you have a really good understanding that getting your temper under better control is important for your own future so you can get married and have children who are not afraid of you.

Your parents will be able to help you to further your rugby career and I think that you may find moments when that fieriness is really useful on the pitch. You were clear that the coach sees the passion in you and although you sometimes get mad, you channel it into the game and never get into fights. You hadn't really thought of this as having self control but you do. Your parents have already booked you onto a rugby camp in the holidays because they understand how important it is for you to develop your rugby skills to the next level. They have also said that your band can practise at your house (very brave of them!) so you will do more music in the week.

You might want to show this letter to your teacher - that will be up to you to decide. As you know, I have sent a copy to your doctor and parents too, so they have it for the future.

Good luck with your ambitions. I think that your ability to talk about problems will really help you in the future. Life can be a challenge for all of us at times but your determination will be a great asset.

Yours sincerely

cc. Parents and GP

EXAMPLE LETTER TO A SCHOOL

Dear Mrs Brown,

I am writing to summarise my work with Raj and to suggest some strategies that might help. I have met with her twice and had a discussion with you and two meetings with her mum. As you know, Raj finds it very difficult to come into school and her mum was settling her down every day. Raj struggled to manage lots of other ordinary events such as children's trips and parties or visiting friends. The information you gave me indicated that she was able to manage changes in the school day, such as a supply teacher or seating changes. Once she settled, she works well in school and had a nice group of friends. She loves to please you and works hard on her own or in a group.

Abi, Raj's mum, has always been aware that Raj was quite anxious around new experiences, right from toddlerhood. She needed support from Abi to settle into them but she was sociable and wanted to join in activities with other children. Raj had had very stable care from her mum but lost her grandmother who had been one of her main carers until she was six. Although this was three years ago, the loss is still very painful for Raj and her mum. It was an unexpected and sudden death, which Raj did not understand at the time. Since then, she has been worried about the same thing happening to her mum.

We used some techniques drawn from Personal Construct Psychology to look at what Raj thought she was like before her grandmother's death and how she sees herself now. We then looked at the kind person she wants to become. Raj was not aware that she had been anxious before her grandma died. She saw herself as having no problems with worrying before her death and thought that she was fine with new experiences. Raj is aware of how anxious she is now and she was able to explain that she does not like being away from her mum because she is worried that Abi might die. By staying near her, she can be sure that it is not happening. This is hard because Raj does like to be with her friends and enjoys social experiences with other children. When she has dealt with being separated from her mum at the start of the school day, Raj does not think about her until it comes towards home time. Then she starts to worry that Abi might not come to collect her. She knows that her grandma had a problem with her heart that no-one was aware of and Raj worries that the same could apply to her mum.

Raj also knows that she has to go to school to learn and she wants to do well in her work. Raj told me that her grandma was very proud of how well she did in school and she wants to do well for her grandma. This is why she always gets into school on normal days, despite it being difficult. Raj feels that school trip days are optional because there are always a couple of children who do not go and she had thought that this was because they did not want to go. You have explained to Raj that this is not the case - the trip is part of school learning and there is work related to the trip. The only children who do not go on trips are those who had an important appointment or needed more supervision than the staff could provide. Raj has said that she will come on trips in the future and Abi is pleased that she has understood why she needs to be there.

Raj is ambitious for her future and part of this is related to her wish to "do Grandma proud". She wants to get a good job, ideally in an office where she has to wear smart clothes and earns lots of money. Raj would like to be an adult who goes out with friends and has a strong relationship with her mum. She wants to be someone who drives and takes her mum out shopping and to the cinema. Raj and her mum both love films. They try to watch all new films at the cinema and they do their own rating afterwards in terms of how entertaining it was, whether the story was a good one and what they thought of the ending. We were able to use this interest to help Raj to think about her own story and what she could do to move towards her ambitions.

We used the idea of writing a film script to help Raj to think how her difficulties could be addressed so that she could get to the part of her film that is about her ambitions for adulthood. She gave three main suggestions:

1. "Meet with friends more."

2. "Go to school with a friend's mum sometimes."

3. "Go on the class trips and write a trip rating report afterwards."

It seems that she can get a lift to school with a friend's mum but she has been reluctant because she knows her mum likes to take her in. When I discussed this with Abi, this was in case Raj got upset when she arrived in school and the friend's mum would have to help her settle. Raj told me that when she went to school with her friend in the past, she was fine and felt less anxious, although she was unsure why this should be the case. She agreed that she might be enjoying being with her friend and is distracted, so does not think so much about how she is feeling. As a result of this discussion, Abi is trying to make a regular arrangement with Raj's friend's mum for Monday and Friday mornings. Her friend's mum is aware of the issues and had offered to help.

From my discussions with Raj and with Abi, they both found the moment of separation difficult. It was a bit easier when her older sister was also going to your school because the girls would walk into the building together. When her sister left for secondary school, Raj found the separation increasingly difficult. Abi was concerned not to leave her in school for the teachers to settle because she is aware that they are busy. You told me that you are very happy to have a system in school to meet and greet Raj and get her into class through giving her some jobs to do for you. Abi will help her to find a friend to walk into the building with and she will leave her at the gate. Abi feels that this will work better because when she goes into the cloakroom with Raj, she tends to cry. Abi did wonder whether this could be connected with feelings about her grandma because in her first two years her grandma took her to school each day and took her into the cloakroom to help with her coat etc. This was what all the parents did at that age so it was not unusual. As the class has moved up, parents have tended to leave their children at the door or at the gate. Abi has not felt able to do that because she was very conscious of the significant loss of Raj's grandma. After her mother's death, Abi rearranged her work hours so that she could drop Raj off at school.

When I met with Abi, she was delighted to hear about the strategies Raj suggested. She felt that as Raj was making the suggestions, she would definitely follow them. It was clear that Abi and Raj are still adjusting to the impact of Grandma's death and they might benefit from some help. Abi made some enquires and she told me that they are going to be sent an appointment to start counselling in the next few weeks. This will probably be after school on a Tuesday. Abi has also talked to Raj about the condition her mum had which meant she could clear up some of the worries about how Raj interpreted Abi's occasional migraines. Raj had thought that they were symptoms of the same condition as her grandma because she could remember her grandma saying that Raj was "giving her a headache". Raj had not understood that this was a figure of speech - Grandma said it most when Raj was talking a lot and she had to concentrate. Raj was reassured that the headaches were nothing to do with a deterioration in Abi's health.

Raj and Abi are aware that the next phase of her development will involve more independence and they both want that to go well. Abi will try to make sure she has more time with her friends and she is looking for some clubs for her to go to. She will definitely start Brownies next month and she is also interested in going to something on a Saturday, perhaps a theatre or dance group.

In terms of support in school, it seems that your ideas for the start of Raj's day will really help with that transition. You also thought that you could develop the trip report idea for the rest of the class, with Raj collating the results. This would give Raj a useful role at the start of trips so that Raj does not have to wait and focus on the separation from her mum. It sounds as if you have plenty of jobs she would be able to help you with on trip days. Raj would particularly like the chance to have a clipboard and pen and you are going to explore Raj getting the children's views of the trip before it starts as part of her report.

I expect that the journey for Raj will not always be smooth but that you and Abi will be able to work well together to address problems as they arise. It is extremely helpful that that she has such positive relationships with you both.

Yours sincerely

cc. Parent and GP

EXAMPLE CONSULTATION SUMMARY

I f you have a single session consultation, you will need to write in proportion to that and you will probably want that to be available quickly. This is easier to do using a standardised format, such as in this example.

∾

Child's name: Marcus Bosko

- **School year: 9**
- **Date of consultation: 29/10/2019**
- **Therapist: Heather Moran, Consultant Child Clinical Psychologist**

Reason for the consultation

Marcus' tutor, Mr. Green, had expressed concerns about Marcus struggling with relationships with other students. He tends to spend most of his time alone, either walking around the building or sitting in the library. Marcus moved to this school at the end of last year and he has not made any strong friendships. I had a single session consultation, first having a talk with Marcus and then with his tutor.

Discussion with Marcus

When I discussed this with Marcus he was very clear that he was not unhappy with his lack of connection with other young people in school. Marcus told me that he was much happier in this school than his last one. He moved from there because he was bullied for what he said was "not fitting in with the cool kids - they made my life a misery". He told me that he has "learnt to keep away" rather than "be near enough to hear them insult or comment about me". Marcus said that he has no wish to be like those young people because "they are shallow and never think about anything except how they look to other people". Marcus sees himself as being the opposite to them, "I never think about how I look. I am too busy to do that - it would take time from thinking about other things". He enjoys spending a lot of time reading and thinking about issues related to climate change and how it could be slowed. Marcus is very interested in the movement against climate change and reads various blogs and websites related to this. He does not discuss this interest with his peers but he does talk to his parents about it. Marcus seemed to be well-informed about a number of issues. He talked about the impact of flying, plastic use and recycling which he has learned from the internet and TV documentaries.

Marcus said that he is aware that his difference from others sets him outside social groups. He does attend Scouts and enjoys it but he does not go to any other social events with young people. He is a regular attender at the local library and would be interested in getting more involved with the library because it fits well with his strong views on recycling. Marcus does not buy any new books himself.

Plan

When Marcus and I had a discussion with Mr. Green, he felt that he might be able to explore a couple of options to help Marcus to engage more with some other students. The science and pastoral team are setting up a recycling education club next term and Marcus is willing to go along to that. The club's role will be to inform the school about issues they could address in order to reduce waste. The science tutor and a pastoral lead will work with the students so the social environment will be well supervised. Marcus felt that "there won't be any cool kids there - they don't have such passions" so it will be safe for him to attend. He was delighted with the offer of being a researcher for that group and said that he will get started with looking at some of the issues to do with paper use in school. The science tutor is willing to mentor Marcus in his research.

The second idea is for Marcus to work with the librarian to run the library. This will mean helping with cataloguing and deciding what books should be showcased each month. There is a small team of student book reviewers who already meet with Mrs. Hart after school on a Thursday. Marcus is willing to attend this group and is very interested in reviewing non-fiction. He already knows Mrs. Hart because she is his English teacher. Marcus is keen to show that "non-fiction reading is just as valuable".

Mr. Green was reassured that Marcus is not unhappy or lonely and Marcus agreed that he is feeling "fine" about coming to school and that is partly related to the building's large indoor spaces. He does not need to go out at break times and he feels it is "safer for geeks like me". Mr. Green made it clear that Marcus could go to him any time he has a problem and Marcus agreed that he would do that.

BECOMING EXPERIENCED

CONTINUING PROFESSIONAL DEVELOPMENT

I have tried to present my own ideas about using a PCP approach in therapy. It will not be the only way and you will develop your own style over time and experience. I would highly recommend finding a PCP community of some kind so that you learn from other people. If you don't have anyone local, then there are some online communities on Facebook. I would also suggest that finding ongoing professional development and supervision would be really helpful if you want to learn more. This book has assumed that you have some knowledge of PCP theory but if you have none so far, you could read the books or find a training course through the links in the Resources chapter.

Remember that if you are interested in hearing more from me, you can send an email with an idea to me: drawingtheideal-self@icoud.com and I will see whether I can write something to design a technique to help. If you have found my book useful, it would be great if you would add a review to the site you bought it from. If there is anything you would like to tell me about your experience, I'd be happy to hear from you.

I wish you well on your therapy journey and I hope it proves to be as interesting and exciting as mine has been so far.

RESOURCES - READING
AND CONNECTIONS

BOOKS

I f you would like to read more about the theory of PCP, a starting point is Kelly's short book: **A Theory Of Personality. The Psychology Of Personal Constructs (2013)** (see below). However, you don't have to start there. My own contact with PCP began in the early 1980s when I was first a teacher. I was shown how to use Tom Ravenette's version of Kelly's repertory grid technique by somebody who was training as an educational psychologist at Birmingham University. I tried it out with the young person and found it so useful. I went onto the same professional training course myself a year later and my tutor, Brian Roberts, was a big fan of PCP. He introduced me to the idea of using PCP approach *whatever* I was doing. It was as useful for working with a child, a family, a teacher, an organisation or for thinking about myself. I then read around various books and articles but I only read the two thick volumes of Kelly's whole theory **The Psychology of Personal Constructs** (see below) when I was doing an advanced course in PCP a few years later. I am glad to have read it and I still regularly use Kelly's original work. It's probably not the best starting point but it is the backbone of all the work described here. I came to PCP theory because I could see that techniques worked and my first PCP learning was through talking to other people about what they were doing. I have added some internet groups and places you can find people with interests in PCP so you can find other people.

~

Ravenette, A.T. (1999). Personal Construct Theory in Educational Psychology: A Practitioner's View. London: Wiley.

https://amzn.to/31E7Nar

This is a classic text for working with young people. The title suggests that it would only be useful to educational psychologists, but this is not the case at all. This book has papers which will be relevant to lots of different professions and it is specific to working with children and young people, their parents and their teachers.

~

Charles Butler and David Green (2007): The Child Within: Taking the Young Person's Perspective by Applying Personal Construct Psychology, 2nd Edition.

https://amzn.to/31IhiW8

A really useful and practical book. Like Tom's book, this has examples and tools that you can try out in your own practice.

~

Moran, H. (Ed.) (2014). Using Personal Construct Psychology with Children and Adolescents.

(iBooks link and Issuu link)

This free ebook gives lots of illustrations of casework from various professionals working with children and young people. It is downloadable from iTunes or from ISSUU (in a format you can read on the computer screen).

∾

Coventry Foundation Guide to Personal Construct Psychology:
2018 Edition. Coventry Constructivist Group.

https://amzn.to/2BzFway

This book is based on the 5 day foundation course in Personal Construct Psychology which is run on an annual basis in Coventry. The course is taught by Diane Allen, Peter Cummins, Heather Moran, Sally Robbins and Grant Weselby. Although this book was initially designed to be used with our course because it provides reading materials which are then expanded in course sessions, it can be used as a brief introduction to Personal Construct Psychology.

∾

George A. Kelly (2013): A Theory Of Personality. The
Psychology Of Personal Constructs.

https://amzn.to/2Pgk7v8
This is the short version of Kelly's theory.

∾

George A. Kelly (2013): The Psychology of Personal Constructs
(Volumes 1 & 2). Routledge.

The full theory and lots of examples. Please note that the language and style are of its time (the original edition was 1955) but this does not prevent it being such a useful book.

Vol. 1: https://amzn.to/363iKFZ
Vol. 2: https://amzn.to/2PkpeKC

∽

Personal Construct Theory and Practice

A free online journal:

http://www.pcp-net.org/journal/journal2017/welcome.html

∽

My own writing

There are links to my own writing on my website: drawingtheidealself.co.uk.

FURTHER TRAINING AND CPD

It is important to remember that the style of PCP therapy will differ for every therapist. There is plenty of space for us all to develop our own techniques, to use each others' ideas and methods and to draw on materials from other modes and models. PCP has not been packaged and monetised in the way that other therapies have been (e.g. CBT, DDP, EMDR). This is probably because there is no fixed way to 'do' PCP therapy and therapy is not its only use.

A PCP approach can so usefully be taken in all sorts of work - working with change and problems in organisations; working in design and architecture; teaching and research. It is just as helpful for understanding why a business is failing as it is to shed light on why a person is so worried all the time. This versatility is so useful that PCP therapists would be unlikely to encourage the limitations of being packaged and marketed. In my view, PCP's niche market is that it is *the* approach for understanding and helping with entrenched, tricky and painful problems. It will allow us to understand some of the most reviled people in society, or the ability of dictatorships to survive, or the reasons governments might ostracise only some of their people.

PCP is also a theory that encourages experimentation and independence. PCP techniques are generally freely available, aside from the purchase of a book or journal. They are offered in the spirit of the theory - here is something you might find useful - try it and pass it on to others if you find it helps.

~

If you are interested in learning more about PCP, there is a Foundation Course in the UK which provides the basics of the theory and teaches some techniques. It is held in Coventry, a city in the centre of England with good transport links by air, rail and road. To find out more, have a look at the Coventry Constructivist Centre's website, http://covpcp.com. Quarterly PCP study days, occasional courses and workshops are also held in Coventry. The Coventry Constructivist Centre is a non-profit organisation so everything offered there is made as affordable as possible.

~

There are conferences and courses in Europe and across the world which bring PCP practitioners together. There are a number of useful links to these on the Kelly Society's website: http://www.kellysociety.org/calendar.html and on the Coventry Constructivist Centre's links webpage: http://covpcp.com/links.html. There is also a Facebook group https://www.facebook.com/CoventryPCP/.

~

ICP International Lab (The International School of Personal Construct Psychology) is an exciting project supporting people who are working with Personal Construct Psychology (PCP), or who are interested in constructivist approaches and looking for development opportunities. https://www.icp-intlab.org/our-project/ It produces an online magazine and a blog.

∾

The Serbian Constructivist Association
http://www.ukons.org.rs/index1_e.htm

∾

EPCA (European Personal Construct Association)
https://www.facebook.com/groups/102639179882305/
http://www.pcp-net.org/europe/home.html

∾

Irish Constructivist Psychology Association. Try the email address through this website: http://www.psychotherapycouncil.ie/members/disciplines/constructivist-therapy/ (Their website is no longer available.)

∾

PCP Association (PCPA) http://www.personalconstructuk.org
PCPA also has a You Tube channel.
https://www.youtube.com/channel/
UCjtLWUpdhhxO3YcU3TmqMAg/videos

∾

The Italian Institute of Constructivist Psychology
https://www.facebook.com/
ScuolaPsicoterapiaCostruttivista/videos/10160508396735368/

∾

Australasian Personal Construct Group
http://kellysociety.org/apcg/about.html

~

Constructivist Psychology Network (formerly North American Personal Construct Network)
http://www.constructivistpsych.org

The Centre for Personal Construct Psychology (UK)
http://centrepcp.co.uk/

~

This is a list of contact details across the world:
http://www.pcp-net.org/europe/countries.html

DRAWING THE IDEAL SELF - ABRIDGED MANUAL

The aim of this book is to provide information and full instructions to professionals who want to use Drawing the Ideal Self (Moran, 2000). Drawing the Idea Self is based upon the theory of Personal Construct Psychology (PCP), developed by George Kelly in 1955 and used in clinical, social and occupational settings to guide clinical practice and as a research tool. It does not require knowledge of PCP to use this technique, although I would hope that it might inspire you to find out more. If you go to my website, you will be able to find links to other PCP sites and find more reading:

drawingtheidealself.com.

If you have questions or ideas related to this technique, you can email me. I am always pleased to hear from people who have tried the technique and I will try to be helpful:

drawingtheidealself@icloud.com.

For more information about PCP, look at the websites in the further reading section.

∽

A very brief explanation of PCP

Kelly (1955) proposed that the theory of PCP applies to everyone, not just to 'clients' with 'problems'. At the time, that was quite a radical proposal. In a nutshell, the theory is that we each have unique, personal theories of life (called constructs) which are based upon our own experiences, and we behave in ways which make sense according to our personal theories. Kelly proposed that we actively interpret (i.e. construe) our experiences, making sense of them in the ways we know how, and they are always open to other interpretations by other people. They are also open to own reconstruction - such as when we decide that a best friend is actually not the person we thought they were.

Kelly suggested that we each have many theories (constructs) and we carry on our lives as if our theories are truths, rather than interpretations. This makes a lot of sense because to reconsider (reconstrue) at every turn would make life impossibly slow and complex. For example, if we had to decide each time we came across a person whether they were dangerous, we'd be stressed by the effort it would take. We are generally happy enough to use short cuts, such as a theory that people at work are usually safe, people who are with children are usually safe, elderly people are usually safe etc. Using these theories (constructions) is good enough for almost every occasion. The exceptions are interesting and surprising. In fact, when we notice exceptions we are expressing a theory very clearly. "I'm amazed that an 80 year old is a murderer!" tells us that the we have a clearly defined theory about 80 year olds and what they don't do. We complain about or celebrate the things that don't fit our constructions. We might tell a friend that we saw a child of three playing a tune on the piano, demonstrating our theory that the piano is difficult to play, that three year olds are not usually capable of such a feat, and that others are likely to share these constructions (or we wouldn't have mentioned it). That's a big theory wrapped up in a little sentence: "There was a brilliant three year old playing Love Me on the TV last night!"

Another important aspect of Kelly's theory is the idea that we construe our experiences in terms of what they are *AND* what they are not. However, we don't often bother to explain what something isn't. If we tell a child to be good at school we might mean 'don't fight, do your work and don't be cheeky'. We generally assume that people are on our wavelength and share our constructions. We sometimes discover that they don't, and then we realise that a word can have different meanings to different people. If the child says "But I *was* good!" on the day he has done no work, we realise that the child's construction of 'good' was not as elaborate as ours. We have a misunderstanding of each other which could be very problematic.

Sometimes we cannot see the sense in another's behaviour and attitudes so those people are problematic to us. In daily life we would usually describe them as *having* the problem, rather than the problem being our inability to see 'sense' in what they do. For example, "She has a dreadful problem with her temper!" could mean "I cannot work out when she is going to get really angry!" or "I can't understand why things annoy her so much!".

Another really important idea in PCP is that we are able to construe someone else's constructions. For example, we will be able to make a reasonable guess about how a good friend might interpret an experience. We are able to construe that person's constructions (theories) and imagine whether they would like a film we saw or whether they might like to borrow the book we have just read. In PCP, saying that we 'know' someone means that we can construe the way they construe. We might not agree with them and we don't have to share their interpretations, but we understand what sense they are likely to make of things. This is why we could say, "Oh, I know her! She is a pain in the neck!" Knowing and liking are not the same, although with friends we might assume that they are.

Drawing the Ideal Self is a way of trying to discover the 'sense' in the young person's behaviour and attitudes (i.e. to understand their construing). It is based upon Kelly's theory and in PCP terms it may be viewed as a technique to elaborate a self characterisation. The emphasis is upon trying to understand a person through understanding the way the person construes him or herself.

Although Kelly's Psychology of Personal Constructs (PCP) was published in 1955, there have only been a few books illustrating a PCP approach to working with children and adolescents (see my website for a reading list). The aim of this book is to add another technique to the therapist's tool box.

∾

An explanation of my terms

I will refer here to 'young person' but please understand that this is unrelated to age so it includes children and young adults too. I will refer to 'interviewing' young people rather than 'talking' with them. To me, interviewing a child is a very purposeful activity, aiming to explore views and to develop understanding. I will also refer to 'therapy' as any work on ideas, feelings, and behaviour which helps to address the problems posed by the young person. I will use the term 'therapist' for the professional person who tries to help the child in a school, clinic, home or youth work setting. All of these are to help the text to flow.

∾

About me

I am a consultant child clinical psychologist and I have been working with children with psychological problems since 1979, in various guises (residential social worker, teacher, foster carer, educational psychologist and clinical psychologist) with the vast majority of my work being as a practising psychologist working with children and families. I use Personal Construct Psychology in all areas of my everyday work.

∾

Equipment

Very little equipment is needed for Drawing the Ideal Self. The therapist and child each need a black pen to ensure that the finished pictures are easily photocopied in case the child wants to take them home. The only other equipment is three sheets of A4 paper. For the first two parts of the technique, the paper needs to be in portrait orientation. For the third part (the rating scale), the paper should be in landscape orientation. At first, the therapist may wish to have the step-by-step instruction sheet available as a prompt (available as a separate download from my website).

The setting

Care needs to be taken with the environment, making sure that there is equality between therapist and child, and that the task can be completed without interruptions. It is vital that the process is allowed to develop its own flow during the session, so a quiet, private place is essential. Allow an hour to complete the whole process but bear in mind that some children will need to complete the task in chunks. There are three natural parts to the process, so the child might have three separate sessions if it cannot be completed in one go. It is best to complete chunks rather than to halt at the point the time runs out, so note how time is passing and make any breaks fit with the chunk points. Experience suggests that most children are able to complete the task in one session, providing the therapist keeps to task too. It can be very tempting to explore issues as they arise in the process but it is much better to wait until the task is completed. Make a mental note of things you might like to return to, and wait until the whole task is complete.

The seating positions in this exercise are important. This is a shared, co-operative task involving taking turns with the child. It involves the sharing paper, ideally without moving it much. Therefore, the best seating position is at right angles to the child, at a desk or table. If the child is right-handed, the best place for the therapist is to sit on the left of the child. This makes it easier to observe the child drawing without it being too intrusive. It also allows the child to read what the therapist has written without having to turn the paper around completely.

~

Rationale

A child never enters this type of interview situation as an entirely unknown person. The therapist will have others' constructions of the child from their referral, whether that came in the form of a chat about the child or a written referral. Drawing the Ideal Self is a way of helping the child to express his personal views about himself, in an effort to address this imbalance. Adults would not tolerate being defined (construed) entirely by other people, but adults do not always afford children the same respect. This technique helps children to have a say about their own development, both how it has been and how they would like it to proceed. This can run parallel to adults' views on similar matters, and can shed light upon why the child is not developing in the ways adults might expect, prefer or hope.

The aim of Drawing the Ideal Self is not to focus on problems, but to gently explore the child's construction of the *'kind of person they would not want to be like'* and the contrasting *'kind of person they would like to be like'*. The purpose is to gain an understanding of how the child feels he compares to *his* ideal self. This provides a very personal measure of self esteem. However, the task avoids asking direct questions about the self until later in the process.

It is important that the therapist does the writing. Children are more likely to use more limited vocabulary and provide less information if they know they will be writing what they have to say, so the task is designed to remove this restriction. The therapist's job here is to provide the role of scribe, writing what the child says and using their words without interpretation. It is essential that the child's words are transcribed exactly because otherwise their personal meanings will be lost. This way, the child is also free to use words in his personal ways, which is particularly useful when working with children with autism spectrum disorder and language disorders. If the child does use unexpected combinations of words or invented words that are similar to real words, the therapist can simply ask what they mean by what they say. For example, one child described the kind of boy he wanted to be like as "kindful" and "superstitious". He was asked to explain his meanings in a way which did not suggest that he was incorrect in his use of language, something which was crucial to helping him to feel comfortable with the process: *That's interesting, what do <u>you</u> mean by kindful, because everyone has their own meanings of words?* This child said that kindful meant "very kind" which might have been guessed accurately. The child's explanation of superstitious was less expected: he said, "Like a super boy" and then explained the role of a super-hero. Although his use of the word was idiosyncratic, it could be understood by asking him to explain and did not cause a problem once I knew what he meant.

The chapters which follow take the reader step-by-step through Drawing the Ideal Self. It will include instructions and explanations so that the reader can try it out. I recommend that the first trial is of the reader on themselves, then on someone who is not a client. This will allow the therapist to experience the technique from both views and decide whether it valid and is something they want to use, and to develop some proficiency in its use. The example here is clearly a girl but all instructions are clearly modifiable for male and female children.

Initially, the child is asked to explore the kind of person they do *not* want to be like. This is deliberate: it is more difficult to think about changing in the future if there is no baseline to move from. This way, the child elaborates the less desired pole of the construct first, and each step finds (elicits) new constructs. During the process, constructs will be elicited about relationships with family, friends and education. There will be illumination of the child's personal theories about child development and the way in which childhood experiences are connected to opportunities in the future. The child will also be asked to talk about something they fear could interfere with their progress towards the kind of person they would like to be like.

The child can be introduced to the technique with something like this explanation:

I would like to get to know you better so that I can get a better idea of how to help you. I'd like to know how you want to be in the future and then I can see how I can help you get there. I will ask you to do some quick sketches and I will do some writing. Are you willing to have a go?

Step 1: The non-ideal character

(See Fig. 1 below for a completed example.)

In the first step of Drawing the Ideal Self, the child is asked: ***First think about the kind of person you would not like to be like. This is not a real person, but someone from your imagination.*** The therapist writes *The kind of person I would not like to be like* at the top of the page. The child is invited to ***make a quick sketch of the kind of person you would <u>not</u> like to be like in the middle of this page.*** There are lots more pictures to go on the page, so the initial sketch cannot take up the whole page. It helps to indicate where and how much space you would like the child to use. Sometimes children want to draw very detailed pictures but they should be encouraged to sketch (meaning draw a quick picture, not a work of art). Coloured pens are not offered because some children will take a long time making decisions about colour, trying to mix colours to get the right shade or colouring in small details. This would make the task take a lot longer and it is not necessary for the purpose of eliciting constructs.

It is important that the gender of the characters the child draws is decided by the child, so the use of person rather than boy or girl can be helpful. Sometimes the two characters are opposite genders, or one character is the opposite gender to the child. This makes it possible for gender roles or sexuality to be an issue which is expressed and emerges naturally from the process. It is also possible that the characters will not be human, although they will be given personalities. For the purpose of Drawing the Ideal Self, this is not a problem. The therapist must 'go with the flow' from the child, showing curiosity rather than surprise so that the child is not put off. Sometimes it will be necessary to wait until the whole task is complete before drawing attention to surprising elements such as gender or sexual differences. Construing oneself in terms of gender is part of core construing, so it is likely to be an important issue to follow up if the child indicates that he would like to be very like the opposite gender.

After the character is drawn, the child is asked **What kind of person is this? How would you describe this person you wouldn't like to be like?** The therapist writes the child's descriptions next to the sketch, as in Figure 1. Encourage the child to think of three or so descriptions and take care to write exactly what the child says. Do not change the child's grammar because you might inadvertently alter the child's meaning. It is easiest to write these descriptions in bullet point format. If the child gives only physical descriptions, ask him **What kind of person is he/she? What is their personality like?** If no psychological constructs are given after that, just continue using whatever descriptions the child gives. There are some children to whom physical descriptions are very important and may imply other constructs which are psychological. For example, a child with an eating disorder might give constructs *fat, ugly and heavy* to describe the kind of person he would not like to be like. Later (but not now because the flow of this exercise would be lost), each of those constructs could be explored in more detail, leading to other psychological constructs. For example, asking *What are fat people like?* could lead to *lonely and miserable*. The aim of Drawing the Ideal Self is to produce a complete portrait, working through from start to finish. We can always return to explore things in more detail later in the session, or in a further session.

Now details are gradually added to build up a picture of this person the child would <u>not</u> like to be like. This will be done through a number of further questions. The child will be asked to provide details of this imaginary person's lifestyle. In each case, the child will be asked to draw something to illustrate the answer to the question. The complete picture of *the kind of person I would not like to be like* will be made up of a number of small, labeled sketches. These will explore the child's life at home and school, her fears, and her theories about past development and predictions for the future. The sketches will be drawn around their main drawing of the person. When the pictures are finished, they will be compared and this is much easier to do if the additional sketches are in similar positions on the page. I usually work anticlockwise, from a nine o'clock position, with the final part being written at the top of the page. This results in a layout as shown in Figure 1. The order of these elements of the character is not fixed, except for the initial three descriptions and the final two items, History and Future. These need to come at the end of the process because the charcterisation needs to have been be developed for those parts to make sense. Just remember the order you have used and keep to it for the second picture in the process.

~

Bag

The exploration of the person's behaviour and constructs begins with asking about the contents of that child's bag. This is deliberately chosen: all children need a school bag and its contents will reflect their interests, preferences and personal constructs. The child is asked to draw (under the title *Bag*) this person's bag and its contents with something like: *Everyone has a bag: what would a girl like this have in her bag? Remember she is the kind of girl you wouldn't like to be like who is …. (insert constructs from the child's description). Sketch her bag and what she has in it here.* Point to the place on the page where you want the child to draw. Depending on the child's drawing ability, you may need to label the items in the bag but if you do this in a matter of fact manner the child will not be aware that it is because their drawings are unclear. I would usually say, something like, *ok, so let me jot down what she has* and write them next to the drawings. This does not draw attention to why you are labelling them.

～

Birthday present

Next, the child is asked to develop this imaginary girl's character by suggesting a present this person would like for her birthday. This is an important part of a child's life and an opportunity to express character. The kind of person who would like a gun might be very different from the one who would like a Barbie doll. Write another title, *Birthday Present,* and ask the child to **think again about the kind of girl you would not like to be like, and sketch a present she would like.** Indicate to the child to draw under the title. Ask the child why she would like that present and write the answer next to his sketch.

～

Family

The next task is to set this imaginary girl in the context of a family. Ask the child to **draw something to show how a girl like this gets on with her family** underneath a new title *With Family*. Ask the child to explain her sketch and write what she says next to the drawing.

～

Friendships

All children will have some social relationships with other children. They may or may not have friends but all children relate to others with varying degrees of success. Write the next title *With Friends* and ask the child **how would a girl who is ......(insert constructs) get on** *with friends? Sketch something to show what she is like.* Write the child's description next to her drawing.

～

Greatest fear

Now write the title *Greatest Fear*. Say to the child something like *Everyone is afraid of something. What would a girl like this be afraid of? Draw her greatest fear here.* Ask the child why this kind of girl would be afraid of what she has drawn and write down what she says. This may reveal common fears (like spiders) or fears more connected with the character of the girl he does not want to be like (like being shot by a rival gang).

～

History

The next area to explore the child's understanding of the development of this girl she does not want to be like. This often brings up some interesting theories about influences, determinism, fate and the importance of experiences. Write the title *History* and ask the child to tell you *How did this ...(insert constructs) girl get to be like this? Was she born like this or did something happen to make her like this? Tell me what you think?* Write down, word for word, what the child says.

～

Future

Finally, explore the child's views about how a person's character interacts with their past to leads to their future. The child is asked, *What kind of future will this person have? How will things work out for her?* Write down what the child says under the title *Future*.

This question often illuminates the possibilities the child faces if she does turns out to be like this girl she does *not* want to be like. It can reveal the fears of the child and perhaps also the threats other people (e.g. parents or teachers) may have made in an effort to motivate the child to change (such as, "If you carry on like *that* you will end up lonely/in prison/unemployed/dead!").

The final picture should look coherent and complete. Put this to one side, preferably upside down so that it is truly out of sight. This is so that the child will not merely make the most obvious contrast without considering possibilities, working with an exactness which would not necessarily be a more elaborative choice. If the child chooses a contrast which is very obvious then that is fine but we don't want to push them in that direction.

Figure 1. Example of Step 1

Step 2: The ideal character

(See Fig. 2 below for a completed example.)

The next step is to explore *the kind of person I would like to be like*. An example is given in Figure 2. In PCP terms this is means elaborating the contrast pole of the construct. To do this, go through the same steps to create a picture this alternative person which could be described as an ideal self. Say something like, *Now let's have a look at the kind of person you would like to be like. Think about what she might be like. Again, this isn't a real person, but it could be made up of bits of people you have met, or it could be from your imagination.* While the child is thinking, write the title *The kind of girl I would like to be like* at the top of a new piece of A4 paper (in portrait orientation). At the end of the process, these two pictures will be compared, so take care to place items in similar places on the page. Start at the same place on the page as in the first picture and proceed in the same direction (anticlockwise, from 9 o'clock). There is not usually any problem with this. The instructions seem to set up the expectation of a pattern matching the first picture.

Go through the same process as for the first picture, using the same headings. Experience suggests that making the second picture is quicker than the first, with children being more able to construe how the process works and what is expected of them.

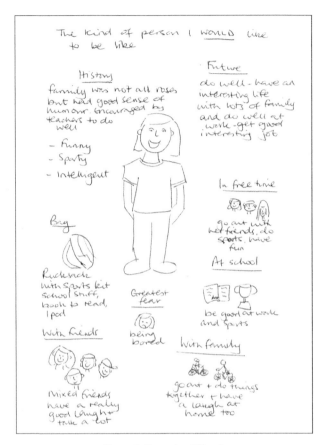

Figure 2: Example of Step 2

Step 2: The rating scale

The last step in Drawing the Ideal Self is an exploration of the child's view of herself. This is the way to find out what the child thinks she is like <u>now</u>, and at various points in time (past and future). The rating scale part of this process is crucial: it connects the two pictures in the exercise. Together, the three pictures make a sensible whole which is rich in information about the child's view of herself. It is a way of the child explaining her development, her ambitions for her development and her experience of movement towards and away from the Ideal Self over time. Later in this part of the process the child is invited to explore her theories about those experiences which have influenced her development. She will be asked about her anticipation of how her development will proceed, and what she and others could do to support her development towards her Ideal Self. First, take the two pictures which have been completed in steps 1 and 2 and place them on the table in front of the child, with *the kind of girl I would not like to be like* on her left, and *the kind of girl I would like to be like* on her right. Take a third piece of A4 paper in landscape orientation and place it in between the two pictures as in Figure 3. Draw a line across that page (linking the two pictures) - this will be the rating scale. Make sure that the line does not go to the edge of the paper because you may need to write above the end points (and it is better for photocopying/scanning).

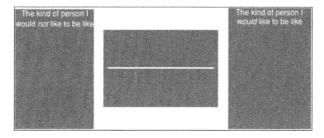

Figure 3: Layout of the three pages, ready for the rating scale

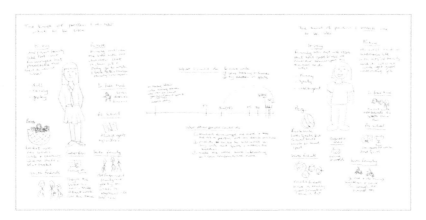

Figure 4: Completed Drawing the Ideal Self

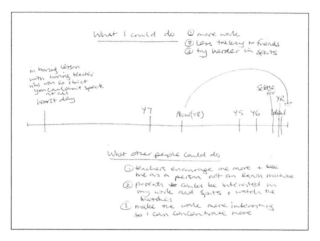

Figure 5: Completed rating scale

xplain this final step to the child: *Now let's get an idea of where you think you are on this scale. We have the kind of girl you don't want to be like here, (point to the picture on the left), and the kind of girl you would like to be like here (point to the picture on the right). Think about what you have been like recently, for most of the time. Put a line like this* (demonstrate a short vertical line which crosses the rating scale) *to show where you usually are.* When the child has drawn their line, write <u>Now</u> above the line. Next, ask the child to rate the place they would like to be: *Where would you like to be on this line, in an ideal world?* Mark this rating <u>Ideal</u>. This is the <u>Ideal Self</u> rating. Notice the difference between the Now and Ideal ratings. Is the child pretty much like they want to be? Is the child a long way away? It is important to remember that this is a self-created scale for that individual child and the distance between points will become clearer as they add additional rating points. Therefore, it will be better to notice the difference and not to comment aloud at this stage.

Encourage the child to consider whether they need to become exactly like their Ideal Self: *If you can't get all the way there, what would you settle for? Put a mark on the line to show what would be ok for you.* Mark this rating <u>Settle For</u>. Some children will insist that this rating is in the same place as their <u>Ideal</u> rating, and others will be able to make another, less extreme point on the scale. If the rating is in the same place, mark it at the same point, writing *Settle For* above the *Ideal* rating. It is interesting to note whether the child will settle for less than perfection in their personal development. The child who aims very high is more likely to experience disappointment with herself and this might be linked with intense feelings of distress (e.g. anger, anxiety, urges to self harm) if she sees herself as failing to be the person she wants to be. In PCP terms, this is a risk of invalidation - her most important theories about the kind of person she wants to be are threatened.

Next, ask the child to **Think about your worst ever day, whenever that was. Where have you been on this scale? Have you ever been more like the kind of girl you don't want to be like?** (*point to the kind of girl she does not want to be like*). **How close have you got to her?** Put a line on the scale. Mark this *Worst Day*. This rating shows how close the child has been to this undesired pole of the construct. It is very interesting to see the child's reaction to this: often I see a wry smile, showing that she is well aware that she is able to move along this construct of self, according to circumstances. Make a comment about the distance, retaining a curious, interested approach e.g. **That's a long way from where you want to be/That's quite close to where you are now./So you have been right down there, exactly the way you don't actually want to be**. Notice the child's response, but do not get involved in a big discussion at this point. The art to this part of the process is to keep going without missing an opportunity to let the child know that you are finding their ratings very interesting.

Now place other points in time on the rating scale. I usually ask children to think in terms of school years because they are naturally defined points in time and schools make much of the differences between the school years. Generally, it is a good to have about half a dozen additional ratings to show progress over time. The aim is for them to rate each point in time as a separate element, so it is helpful to remind the child that ratings will not necessarily show uninterrupted progress towards their ideal. In my experience, children make comparisons thoughtfully. They will move their rating points up (towards their ideal rating) and down (towards non-ideal) without prompting because they recognise that their progress is related to their context.

The decision about which time points to rate is somewhat arbitrary, but within the constraint of being able to show change (or not) over long enough periods. This means that the task can be tailored to the age and experience of the individual child. For a younger child, it is possible to ask her to rate the points such as before school, reception/first school year, and then each year in school to their current year. For older children, ask for a before attending school rating, and then pick time points spread across their school career (e.g. Reception, Year 3, Year 6, Year 7, Year 9). Try to pick times with significance in school careers, such as times which involved adjustment to a change or a particular challenge such as examinations. These are times at which children are overtly construed by teachers and parents often in terms of their psychological characteristics and their academic ability (e.g. as *average, slow, adjusted to school, lazy, confident*). Comparing the 'before school' rating with other ratings allows some evaluation of the impact of moving away from the family and entering school life with new ways of being construed. The therapist might also wish to explore the impact of experiences she thinks are relevant to that child's development, such as an accident, a change of home circumstances or a change in close relationships (e.g. a move into foster care, a road accident, a death). The therapist can use her knowledge of the child's life to decide what to include here. Simply add in some additional rating points, e.g. *Where were you on this line when you went into foster care?* e.g. *Where were you after you came out of hospital?* Depending upon the problem, the therapist may also want to explore how the child thinks others see her. Ask the child to mark where significant others would say she was: *Where would dad say you were? What about mum? Where would your friends put you? Where would your teacher say you were?* It is important to distinguish these ratings from the child's self-ratings. It can help to write the labels for these below the line (rather than above) so that things are clear at a glance. As long as the rating points are clearly labelled there should be no problem even if there are a quite a lot of ratings points on the scale.

When the all the rating points have been placed, take a good look at the total picture. What does it say overall? Is there a large gap between the way the child's view of herself and the way she wants to be? This provides a very personal measure of self esteem. If there is a big difference, we can expect that the child won't feel good about that difference. In contrast, if the child is satisfied with the way she sees herself now, then 'therapy' is unlikely to lead to significant or permanent changes in behaviour. In my experience, those children who have rated themselves as already being like their ideal have remained unaffected by the efforts of other people to change them. They have been comfortable with themselves regardless of the problems other people would see them as having. This was really useful information and served as an excellent predictor of the likelihood of significant changes in behaviour over a few years. In such a situation, I would heed the warning that the child is not seeking therapy and switch clients and work with parents or teachers, working with someone else in the child's network who *is* seeking change.

The rating scale is deliberately uncalibrated, with no numbers on it at all. This allows for personal interpretation of distance between ratings. It means that the child considers distance in relation to points she has placed on the scale rather than being focussed on what a difference between numbers might mean. Therefore, it is not relevant to calculate numerical scores from her ratings. This retains the emphasis on the child's very personal way of construing, without the temptation to compare the scores of two children, or to interpret similarities between children as suggesting something about children in general. This technique is not designed to be norm-referenced and to do so would make it into something different. There is a very good PCP self esteem scale which is norm-referenced (see Bultler & Green, 2007), if that is what you are seeking.

The Drawing the Ideal Self technique will provide a personal rating of the *child's view* of her own self-esteem, where self-esteem is the difference between the way she wants to be and the way she construes herself as being. The interpretation of the difference must be decided in agreement with the child. If the gap between Ideal and Now looks big to you, ask the child what she thinks, e.g. **You seem to**

be a long way from the way you want to be, is that right? Is it diffi-
cult for you not being like you want to be? The reason for asking the
child is that it may not be a problem for her, even if you feel that the
gap would be intolerable. A child may see the distance as expected
or reasonable, and have an anticipation of being able to reach their
ideal without too much difficulty. She might expect that she will
reach it by the time she needs to or that age will necessarily lead to
development in the desired direction. It is interesting to add an additional question about <u>when</u> the child would like to reach that point.
If the gap is large and the child feels that she really wants to reach
that point within a short time frame, then there is a risk that she
could become disheartened and feel a strong sense of failure, in her
own terms.

Do not ignore the *Settle For* rating. This can be as important as the
Ideal. It may be that the child is able to think of an ideal position, yet
feel comfortable with the fact that they may not reach it. Another
child might have their *Ideal* and *Settle For* ratings located in the same
place on the scale. This suggests that there is no flexibility in their
ambitions, but remember to check out with the child whether this is
actually the case. The child might wish to reach the point she will
Settle For within a much shorter time frame than it would take her to
attain the *Ideal* position. Depending upon what this position would
be like (i.e. what the child would be like at this position, how much
change would be required and how much of that is within the child's
control), this could be realistic or problematic.

The next part of Drawing the Ideal Self is to explore movement
between some of the key points on the rating scale, starting with the
difference between the way the child is now and the way she wants
to be. On the rating scale, the therapist connects the two points,
making a link between <u>Now</u> and <u>Ideal</u>. Physically, the connection is
shown by drawing an arc with an arrow between the two. (See the
example in Fig. 5.) Explain to the child that you are interested in this
difference with something like, **Let's have a look at the difference**
between these two. You are here now, (*starting at the <u>Now</u> point,*
drawing an arc over the top of the scale to <u>Ideal</u>)**, and you want to be**
here, at your ideal. Tell me three things other people could do to help

you to get there. Above the arc, write *3 things others can* do and write the three things the child tells you, each with a separate numbered bullet point. Sometimes, I ask the child to tell me something their parents could do, something their teachers could do and something their friends could do to help the child to become more like the person she wants to be. This provides a little more focus but it may not be necessary. If the child says that she can't think of anything, I would write a question mark for that item. It is useful for the therapist to know that the child has no idea *who* can help them to change or *how* they might be helped. It could be very important to let adults (parents/teachers etc) know that the child cannot see a way forward. If the child has a view of what might be done, then intervention is more likely to succeed if it includes the things the child suggests. For example, if the child says that her teachers could help her by giving her better marks for work, it would be helpful if teachers knew this information and could consider the way they give feedback in their marking. Maybe a new marking scheme could be worked out with the child so that she could to get the kind of feedback she needed?

Next, the child will be encouraged to consider her part in determining her own development. Write *3 things I can do* next to the arc between *Now* and *Ideal* and the child to **tell me three things you can do to help yourself get from here** (point to *Now*) **to here** (point to *Ideal*) **and become more like your the person you want to be.** Jot down the child's answers as three separate numbered points. Again, if the child cannot make a suggestion, write a question mark next to the number. This is very important information, perhaps indicating a sense of helplessness.

In my experience, most children are able to come up with ideas about how make changes in their lives and these are often exactly the sort of things adults might suggest to them. This has proved to be very helpful to parents and teachers who can then encourage the child to follow her own plan, rather than telling her to follow their plan. Even though the things the child will be doing are very similar, the sense of agency might make a significant difference to what that feels like to a child, especially to one who has found herself to be in trouble with adults. The child's suggestions might be used as targets, leading to a discussion of how they could be achieved. The suggestions for other people could be used to help them to support the child's movement towards to kind of person he would like to be. The child's own suggestions will have much more meaning and this can avoid adult-dominated contracting which is sometimes tried as a solution to behavioural problems. The child's proper engagement in the process of addressing problems will increase the likelihood of success.

The child will need to give permission for her information to be shared. It is helpful to tell the child that your job is to help people to help her; and that they will be able to do that better if they under-stand her views. Suggest to the child how you might explain this to those people who have made the referral (e.g. parents and teachers). Check whether you will also be able to show the pictures, so it helps them to understand the child's views (this is the most powerful way to explain what has been done). If you are to write a report, it is in keeping with the PCP approach to tell the child what will go into the report and why.

The aim of the following section is to suggest a format for reporting Drawing the Ideal Self. It is not the only way to report, but it might provide a starting point for you try and then you can develop a style which is more to suited your particular style and needs. The first paragraph provides a short and simple explanation of the technique. This may be freely copied if credited. The second part gives an outline of what might be included and what to pay particular attention to.

Explanation of Drawing the Ideal Self for reports

This assessment of (child's name)'s views used a technique called Drawing the Ideal Self (Moran, 2001), which is based upon Personal Construct Psychology (Kelly, 1955). The aim was to explore (child's name)'s personal views of (his/her) own development, particularly focussing upon personal ambitions for (himself/herself) in the future, and the kind of person (he/she) would like to become. The technique used a combination of drawing and dictation to elaborate (child's name)'s views, and a rating scale to provide a very personal measure of self-esteem. It explored the kind of relationships with family and friends that (child's name) would like to have in the future, and how (he/she) would like to get on at school. It elicited (child's name)'s views of the way personal history affects future development, and (child's name)'s fears about what could interfere with (him/her) becoming the kind of person (child's name) would like be. The outcomes of the assessment have been discussed with (child's name) and (he/she) has given permission for these to be shared in this report.

Pictures and constructs

Include the description of the kind of person the child would like to be like, and the kind of person he/she would not like to be like. Make sure that these descriptions are exactly what the child said, rather than your own interpretation. Comment upon how this compares with information from other sources (especially noting major differences) and whether the child's ambitions are likely to be socially desirable.

Summarise the kind of relationships the child would like to have with family, friends, and school. Note anything significant about fears of the kind of person he/she would like to be like. Draw attention to anything which might indicate that the child would prefer to stay as he/she is or to become very different.

Describe any significant the links between the history and future of both characters. Often this is where children show awareness of those life experiences which have not been good for their development.

Rating Scale

Report on the comparison between the self now and the ideal self – comment upon whether there is a large gap between _Now_ and _Ideal_ and whether he/she would settle for anything other than _Ideal_. This is the self-esteem measure and it will need some explanation. If the child is very unlike the way he/she wants to be, it would be reasonable to expect the child to feel at least uncomfortable with their own development. If there is very little difference, then it is unlikely that the child will wish to change their behaviour. In such circumstances it is often more fruitful (i.e. quicker and more likely to work) to work with the carers or teachers, helping them to adjust the way they deal with the child because they are the people who want to see changes. Explain this in the report if the child does not seem to be seeking change and make some suggestions for what might help, based upon what you now know about the child.

Report word-for-word what the child thinks will he/she and others could do to help him/her become more like their _Ideal_. Explain the direction of changes between rating points and the reasons the child gave for the change. If the child is critical of adults in this, it will need some careful handling in the report to avoid polarising the views of both parties. Report any differences between the way the child thinks various people would rate her. Be tactful if the child's ratings might be a surprise to other people.

Conclusions and recommendations

In conclusion, present a summary of the assessment, particularly emphasising whether the child is seeking to change and whether that change would be in the same direction as the adults are seeking. The therapist can then make suggestions for the direction and focus of any further work. Your recommendations will be based upon what you have understood to be the problems and any barriers affecting movement. It is helpful to highlight how the adults can support in ways which will make sense to the child (e.g. Jane wants to be able to show how helpful she can be so allocating her a regular helping role within the class would be useful).

~

Copies

You may want to copy your report to parents and to other professionals. As long as the child is comfortable with them seeing a copy, I would argue that the more people can understand the child, the better they will be able to help him/her.

~

Repeating Drawing the Ideal Self with the same child

Drawing the Ideal Self is not norm-referenced so repeating it is not a problem. The results provide a snapshot of construing about the self and it will show some core construing. Core construing does not change quickly so repeating DiS may not be useful within a short time-frame. Construing will develop in relation to experiences, so points of transition are likely to lead to the development of many new constructs and to the consolidation of some previous construing. For example, moving into secondary education is likely to have a significant impact on the construing of self. Upsetting experiences are likely to lead to significant changes in construing, such as a bereavement or a road accident. In the same way, pleasant surprises and success will have an impact on self-construing (e.g. exam success, winning a competition, performing in a show).

Repeated similar experiences will lead to construing becoming more and more connected to core construing. For example, repeated bullying or repeated failure or success in a particular situation. This applies to the construing of self as a learner of particular school subjects. It would be expected that construing of self would develop and change over time so repeating Drawing the Ideal Self might be really useful after a while. However, unless something has happened to lead to a change in construing, it might not be the best use of time. It is likely to be more useful to use the DiS rating scale and add more ratings to it, using the method described above.

~

Sharing this technique

I am always very happy to hear about how people use this technique and how/where when they find it useful. I have made this technique freely available so that it can be used without concern for the cost. My aim is to further the understanding and support for people who are struggling in some aspect of their lives. The more free techniques there are, the more easily they can be helped. I also believe that professionals should share what we know as much as possible. I have benefitted enormously from the work of experts in the PCP world and I want to be able to make a contribution too. Please do tell other people if you find it helpful and give them a copy yourself or direct them download one from my website.

~

Modifying this technique

You may modify this technique to make a new development of it, but please reference my technique in your own work and provide a link to my website. This is how many so interesting techniques come into being and I would be delighted to hear about any modifications you make, mainly so that I can use them too! If you look on my website, you will find links to published research using variations on Drawing the Ideal Self.

~

Training sessions or publications

This booklet may be used, copied and passed on free of charge, as long as it remains intact, with the cover and all pages included. Selling it is prohibited and that goes against my personal purpose - it must be free. It cannot be used as the main item in any course or training without my permission. However, I am unlikely to deny permission, especially if it is delivered to a public sector service, but I would like to know so that I can see whether professionals are finding it useful. It can be referenced with a link to my website to show people where they can find it: drawingtheidealself.co.uk.

Printed in Great Britain
by Amazon